Barbecue
COOKBOOK

by Mary Jane Finsand

Ideals Publishing Corp.
Milwaukee, Wisconsin

Contents

ISBN 0-89542-617-X

COPYRIGHT © MCMLXXIX BY MARY JANE FINSAND
MILWAUKEE, WIS. 53201
ALL RIGHTS RESERVED. PRINTED AND BOUND IN U.S.A.

Photograph opposite:
Western Ham, p. 28

How to Use Your Barbecue

Barbecuing gives us a whole new dimension in cooking. It can add both versatility and economy to your eating enjoyment.

Before you start barbecuing, always read the manufacturer's instructions, and use them. Time and temperatures used in the recipes in this book will vary if barbecuing is done on a cold or windy day.

Charcoal briquets are probably the most widely used outdoor cooking fuel. There is a wide variety of charcoal briquets; some burn slowly while others burn hotter. Some are designed to give off fruit or wood flavors. With experimentation you will find the type or mixture which will best serve your needs. When using charcoal, heat control is the most important step to learn.

SIMPLE METHODS TO RAISE HEAT TEMPERATURES

Lower grill surface
Tap ashes off coals
Add more fuel (always around edge of bed until hot)
Open dampers on bottom of fire bowl
Use an aluminum reflected surface by tenting (often needed when windy or cold)

SIMPLE METHODS TO LOWER HEAT TEMPERATURES

Raise grill surface
Remove a few briquets
Partially close dampers on bottom of fire bowl

Gas grills are fast becoming the most popular way to barbecue. Their fast starting, quick preheating, and heat control makes them a year-round favorite for outdoor cooking. Always preheat your gas grill on high and cook on medium or low unless otherwise stated.

"Direct heat" means placing the food directly over the briquets.

"Indirect heat" means placing the food over a drip pan and, in gas, a heat resistant surface (see Equipment).

"Moist heat" is gained by adding water to the drip pan. Moist heat allows meat and dishes to cook and brown evenly, and the fat drippings will not burn to the drip pan causing the food to taste burnt.

EQUIPMENT MOST NEEDED WHEN BARBECUING

Fuel
Fire starter
Water
Heavy aluminum foil
Tongs, fork or spatula
Large plate or platter
Brush or baster
Hot pads or mitts
Drip pan (made of aluminum foil or an aluminum pie or cake pan)
Asbestos cement board (for gas grills)

Asbestos cement board comes ⅛ or ¼-inch thick. Buy a piece larger than the bottom of your drip pan and big enough to cover center section of gas jets. The asbestos cement board will be placed directly under your drip pan, not on the gas jets.

EQUIPMENT NICE TO HAVE WHEN BARBECUING

Table near grill
Rotisserie or any accessories for your barbecue
Cutting or carving boards
Casserole dishes (aluminum, ovenproof glass, or red clay pot drip trays)
Picnic table
Special outdoor linen of paper, plastic or fabric
Special outdoor dishes
Great guests for the fantastic food

HOW TO BUILD A FIRE

A successful barbecue starts with a carefully built and controlled fire. Start the fire about 30 to 45 minutes before you want to begin barbecuing. This will allow the charcoal to burn evenly and to develop an intense heat. A charcoal fire may be started with several different methods.

Charcoal briquets are the most efficient. They give a longer, steadier and hotter heat. Briquets should be dry. For best results choose a standard high grade of charcoal or briquets. To start the fire, place twisted newspaper and enough kindling to burn for several minutes on the bottom of the firebox. Cover kindling with charcoal and pile in a pyramid. Ignite paper in several places. Allow time for the fire to burn down to glowing embers.

Another method is to arrange charcoal in a pyramid and then to pour charcoal lighter fluid or commercial rubbing alcohol over it. Soak the charcoal thoroughly, then light with a long match.

A third method is to form a cup from aluminum foil. Fill with 2 or 3 spoonsful of solidified alcohol (sterno) and place on the bottom of the firebox. Add charcoal. Ignite alcohol. Let the charcoal burn to glowing embers. Then spread evenly over bottom of firebox.

COOKERY TERMS

Barbecue: To cook food in the open, whether on a spit or rack over hot coals or in a rotisserie basket, basting often with a highly seasoned sauce.

Baste: To moisten foods during cooking with fat drippings, water, oil or a sauce.

Broil: To cook by direct heat in a broiler or over hot coals.

Brown: To make food a brown color by frying, sautéing, broiling or baking.

Fry: To cook in hot fat. Cooking in a small amount of fat is called sautéing and cooking in a deep layer of hot fat is known as deep-fat frying.

Garnish: To add decorative color with small pieces of colorful food such as pepper, parsley, pimiento.

Marinate: To soak food in a seasoned liquid to tenderize or to add flavor.

Sauté: To cook food quickly with fat, butter or margarine.

Score: To partially cut narrow gashes through outer surface of food.

Sear: To brown meat quickly by intense heat.

OUTDOOR GRILL TIMETABLE

The time required for outdoor grilling will vary depending on the amount of heat, the distance from the flame and construction of the cooking device.

BEEF STEAKS (1 inch thick)
Rare—8 to 12 minutes
Medium—12 to 15 minutes
Well done—15 to 20 minutes

BEEF STEAKS (1½ inches thick)
Rare—10 to 15 minutes
Medium—14 to 18 minutes
Well done—18 to 25 minutes

LAMB CHOPS AND STEAKS (1 inch thick)
Medium rare—6 to 14 minutes
Well done—18 to 25 minutes

LAMB CHOPS AND STEAKS (1½ inches thick)
Medium rare—8 to 16 minutes
Well done—20 to 30 minutes

CHICKEN
Split—25 to 45 minutes

HAM STEAKS
1 inch thick—30 to 35 minutes
1½ inches thick—35 to 45 minutes

HAMBURGERS
Rare—10 to 12 minutes
Medium—14 to 15 minutes
Well done—18 to 20 minutes

FISH STEAKS
1 inch thick—6 to 9 minutes
1½ inches thick—8 to 12 minutes

Beef

MEAT LOAF

2 lbs. ground beef
2 T. dried onion flakes
½ c. bread crumbs
½ c. catsup
2 eggs
Salt and pepper

Combine all ingredients. Place in aluminum foil pan. Serves 6 to 8.

Briquet Covered Cooking Method: Barbecue over indirect heat for 45 to 50 minutes.

Gas Method: Barbecue over medium indirect heat for 45 to 50 minutes.

ROLLED RIB ROAST

Briquet Covered Cooking or Gas Method: Bind one 6 to 8-pound rolled rib roast with a heavy string or butcher's cord. Place on spit, securing with prongs. Turn spit constantly over low to medium heat. Baste with a barbecue sauce and juices from meat. Barbecue until of desired doneness. Cool before carving.

BEEF ROLL-UPS

½ lb. bacon
3 T. finely chopped onion
3 T. finely chopped mushroom
1 t. butter
2 T. chopped parsley
1 t. ground basil
Salt and pepper
8 to 10 thin slices of beef

Grind bacon in meat grinder. Combine bacon, onion, mushroom, and butter in saucepan. Cook for 3 to 4 minutes. Add parsley, basil, salt, and pepper. Cook 2 minutes. Spread bacon mixture on beef slices. Roll up and secure with toothpicks. Place on barbecue over medium heat. Cook 10 to 12 minutes. May be brushed with any barbecue sauce for beef. Makes 8 to 10 servings.

BEEF TENDERLOIN

½ lb. beef tenderloin per person
Salt and pepper or
Herb seasoning

Briquet Covered Cooking Method: Season to taste. Barbecue over high indirect heat. Allow 15 minutes per pound for medium/rare roast.

Gas or Spit Method: Season to taste. Place securely on spit. Barbecue over high indirect heat. Allow 15 minutes per pound for medium/rare roast.

BEEF BRISKET

½ lb. beef brisket per person
Beef Bouillon Marinade, p. 56

Marinate brisket for 1½ to 2 hours. Marinade may be spread on brisket while cooking for added flavor.

Briquet Covered Cooking Method: Barbecue over indirect heat for 2 to 2½ hours.

Gas Method: Barbecue over indirect medium/low heat for 2 to 2½ hours.

PIZZA PATTIES

1 lb. ground beef
¾ c. cracker crumbs
½ c. mozzarella cheese, grated
1 small onion, finely chopped
1 small garlic clove, minced
¼ t. oregano
Salt and pepper to taste
1 egg
¼ c. tomato paste
¼ c. red wine

Combine all ingredients, mixing well. Shape into patties.

Briquet Covered Cooking or Gas Method: Barbecue patties over high direct/indirect heat until of desired doneness.

Photograph opposite:
Beef Roll-Ups

STANDING RIB ROAST

1 lb. rib roast per person
Salt and pepper or
Herb seasoning

Briquet Covered Cooking Method: Season to taste. Barbecue over high indirect heat. Allow 10 to 12 minutes per pound for medium/rare roast.

Gas Method: Season to taste. Barbecue over high indirect heat. Allow 10 to 12 minutes per pound for medium/rare roast.

ROLLED BEEF ROAST

½ lb. rolled rump roast per person
1 t. nutmeg
1 t. salt
⅛ t. pepper
2 to 3 c. red wine

Marinate roast in wine, nutmeg, salt, and pepper 5 to 6 hours.

Briquet Covered Cooking Method: Barbecue over low indirect heat for 2½ to 3 hours. Baste with red wine marinade.

Gas or Spit Method: Place securely on spit. Barbecue over low indirect heat for 2½ to 3 hours. Baste with red wine marinade.

BEEF SHORT RIBS

1 lb. short ribs per person
1 sliced onion
2 bay leaves
Salt and pepper
1½ c. water

Preparation before barbecuing: In heavy skillet, brown meat on all sides. Add remaining ingredients and simmer 1 to 1½ hours. Remove meat and refrigerate. Discard bay leaves. Skim fat from liquid and blend thoroughly.

Briquet Covered Cooking, Flat Grill, or Gas Method: Barbecue over medium direct heat for 45 minutes, turning occasionally. Meat may be basted with onion sauce while cooking for added flavor.

STEAK SUPREME

¾ lb. T-bone steak per person
4 T. favorite steak sauce
2 t. salt
½ t. basil
1 T. water

Score steak slightly on both sides with sharp knife. Mix steak sauce, salt, basil, and water together thoroughly. Rub sauce into both sides of steak using heel of your hand. Allow to rest 1 hour. Barbecue over direct heat for 15 to 20 minutes, turn once.

ITALIAN FLANK STEAK

½ lb. flank steak per person
Italian Sauce, p. 53

Prick or score flank steak. Place in shallow baking dish. Cover completely with Italian Sauce. Marinate 6 to 8 hours or overnight.

Briquet Covered Cooking, Flat Grill or Gas Method: Barbecue over medium direct heat for 40 minutes. Turn once. Meat may be basted with sauce for added flavor.

SHEPHERD MEAT LOAVES

1 lb. pork sausage
1 lb. ground beef
½ c. dry bread crumbs
½ c. shredded Cheddar cheese
1 egg
Salt and pepper

Combine all ingredients and mix well. Place in 8 to 10 individual aluminum foil boats or wrappings. Serves 8 to 10.

Briquet Covered Cooking, Flat Grill or Gas Method: Barbecue over direct heat 8 to 10 minutes.

TOPPING

2 to 3 c. hot, seasoned whipped potatoes
½ slice American processed cheese per boat

Cover each meat loaf with whipped potatoes. Top with ½ slice cheese. Return to grill until cheese slightly melts.

BEEF-VEGETABLE KEBABS

½ lb. beef stew meat per person
1 can small onions, drained
3 carrots (cut in 1-inch segments)
1 green pepper (cut in 1½-inch segments)
10 to 12 cherry tomatoes
1 to 2 potatoes (cut in 1-inch cubes)

Preparation before barbecuing: Place potatoes in ice water 1 hour to prevent discoloration. Alternate chunks of meat and vegetables on skewers. Serves 6 to 8.

Briquet Covered Cooking, Flat Grill or Gas Method: Barbecue over medium direct heat. Baste with favorite sauce. Allow 30 to 40 minutes total barbecuing time.

CHINESE SHORT RIB KEBABS

1 lb. boneless short ribs per person
3 T. soy sauce
1 t. ground ginger
2 onions, chopped
1 12-oz. can pineapple chunks
1 4-oz. can mushroom pieces
1 8-oz. can sliced water chestnuts
1 c. sliced celery
2 T. cornstarch

Preparation before barbecuing: Cut short ribs in half. Place in shallow baking dish. Combine soy sauce, ginger, chopped onions, and juices from pineapple chunks, mushrooms and water chestnuts. Pour sauce mixture over short ribs and marinate, covered, overnight. Turn occasionally. Barbecue according to directions given below. Pour sauce mixture into pan. Add cornstarch. Cook over low heat, stirring gently until sauce thickens. Add pineapple chunks, mushrooms, water chestnuts, and celery. Heat thoroughly. Place ribs in center of large hot platter. Arrange a wreath of rice or noodles around short ribs. Top with sauce. Serve 6 to 8.

Briquet Covered Cooking, Flat Grill or Gas Method: Thread short ribs on long skewers. Barbecue over medium direct heat for 1½ to 2 hours turning frequently.

STEAK KEBABS

½ lb. sirloin steak per person (cut in 1-inch cubes)
½ lb. bacon
¾ lb. mushrooms
Shallots

Wrap each sirloin cube in bacon. Alternately thread wrapped sirloin cubes, mushrooms and shallots on skewers. Serves 6 to 8.

Briquet Covered Cooking, Flat Grill or Gas Method: Barbecue over medium direct heat. Allow 20 to 30 minutes total barbecuing time.

STUFFED STEAK

1 large boneless round steak
Red Wine Marinade, p. 56
1½ to 2 c. dry bread crumbs
½ c. mushrooms and liquid
½ t. salt
2 T. melted butter or margarine

Divide round steak evenly in half. Place in shallow baking dish and allow to marinate in Red Wine Marinade 4 to 5 hours or overnight. Turn occasionally. Remove and dry. Place steak halves together and tie or pin curved edges securely. Combine dry bread crumbs, mushrooms with liquid, salt, and melted butter. Mix thoroughly until bread crumbs are moist. If more moisture is needed add small amount of Red Wine Marinade. Spoon stuffing into center of steaks. Tie flat edge securely. Serves 6 to 8.

Flat Top Grill Method: Place steak on grill and barbecue 3 to 4 inches above briquets. Turn once. Allow 30 to 40 minutes total barbecuing time.

Spit Method: Place in flat spit basket. Barbecue over indirect heat for 40 to 45 minutes.

MUSHROOM BURGERS

1 lb. lean ground beef
½ c. chopped mushrooms
½ t. salt
2 t. chopped chives

Thoroughly drain and dry mushrooms. Combine ground beef, mushrooms, salt, and chives. Mix well. Form into patties. Chill patties thoroughly. Barbecue over direct heat 10 minutes. Turn once. Makes 4 to 5 burgers.

CHUCK STEAK WITH ONION SAUCE

4¾ lbs. chuck steak, 1½ inches thick
Meat tenderizer

ONION SAUCE

3 T. onion soup mix
2 T. sugar
½ t. salt
Dash of pepper
1 T. prepared mustard
¾ c. water
½ c. catsup
¼ c. cider vinegar
1 T. lemon juice

Sprinkle steak with tenderizer per directions on package. Combine all ingredients in Onion Sauce in a saucepan. Simmer, covered, about 10 minutes. Brush steak with Onion Sauce.

Briquet Covered Cooking or Gas Method: Barbecue chuck steak on both sides over high direct/indirect heat until done, 10 to 30 minutes.

BARBECUED TOP SIRLOIN STEAK

3 lbs. top sirloin steak, 1½ inches thick
2 c. Burgundy wine
1 t. onion powder
¼ t. garlic powder
¼ t. black pepper

Place steak in a shallow bowl or pan. Add wine, then sprinkle with seasonings. Cover tightly and marinate overnight in refrigerator, turning once. Serves 4.

Briquet Covered Cooking or Gas Method: Broil slowly on a greased grill approximately 4 inches from medium-high heat, basting occasionally with the wine marinade.

AMERICANA CHUCK ROAST

½ to ¾ lb. chuck roast per person
Beef Marinade, p. 56

Prick beef with sharp fork. Marinate in Beer Marinade for 3 hours.

Briquet Covered Cooking Method: Barbecue over indirect heat for 2 to 2½ hours. Add briquets as needed. No turning needed.

Gas Method: Barbecue over indirect high heat for 45 minutes. Turn heat to medium/low and finish cooking 1 to 1½ hours.

BEEF TERIYAKI

1 t. ginger
1 clove garlic, minced
⅓ c. grated onion
2 T. sugar
½ c. soy sauce
¼ c. water
2 lbs. tender beef, cut into strips

Mix first 6 ingredients together. Pour over beef strips and put in refrigerator, covered, about 2 hours. Drain beef, arrange on skewers. Serve with rice.

Briquet Covered Cooking or Gas Method: Barbecue over high indirect heat, browning meat slowly on both sides until done, about 10 to 20 minutes. Brush with marinade and turn often.

Photograph opposite:
Mushroom Burgers

POLYNESIAN SHORT RIBS

4 lbs. lean beef short ribs
1 c. pineapple juice
⅓ c. soy sauce
¼ c. brown sugar
1 t. ginger

Combine brown sugar, soy sauce, pineapple juice, and ginger. Place ribs in aluminum foil pan and pour sauce over. Marinate several hours. Serves 4.

Briquet Covered Cooking or Gas Method:
Barbecue over direct heat, 2 to 2½ hours, brushing frequently with marinade. Serve with additional heated sauce.

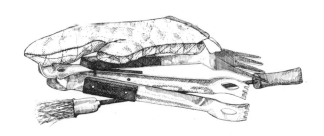

BARBECUE BRISKET

1 3-lb. beef brisket
1 c. catsup
½ c. brown sugar
½ c. vinegar
1 c. water
2 T. prepared mustard
¼ c. minced onion
2 T. butter

Sauté onion in butter; add remaining ingredients. Pour over brisket and marinate overnight. Serves 8.

Briquet Covered Cooking or Gas Method:
Barbecue over low heat 3½ to 4 hours, basting occasionally with marinade.

TENDERED BEEF

1 3-lb. round steak or chuck roast, 2 inches thick
Meat tenderizer
1 5-oz. bottle soy sauce
¼ c. brown sugar, packed
1 T. lemon juice
¼ c. bourbon or brandy
1 t. Worcestershire sauce
1½ c. water

Sprinkle meat with tenderizer per package directions. Combine remaining ingredients. Marinate meat in refrigerator at least 6 hours, turning once.

Briquet Covered Cooking or Gas Method:
Barbecue meat over medium direct/indirect heat to desired doneness. Spoon on marinade often during barbecuing.

STUFFED GREEN PEPPERS

6 medium green peppers
1 15-oz. can chili with meat
1 12-oz. can whole kernel corn, drained
¾ c. catsup
¼ t. Tabasco sauce
¾ c. bread crumbs

Slice top of peppers; remove seeds and membranes. Drop into boiling water, blanch 5 minutes; drain and cool. Place each pepper on heavy-duty aluminum foil. Combine remaining ingredients, mixing well. Divide mixture equally and fill each pepper. Wrap foil around peppers, double fold at top.

Briquet Covered Cooking or Gas Method:
Barbecue packets 6 inches above high direct/indirect heat for 30 to 40 minutes.

Poultry

SECURING THE BIRD ON THE SPIT

Cooking poultry on a slowly rotating spit is an excellent way of preparing chicken, turkey, or several small Cornish hens, for no other method rivals the crispy doneness and golden glow of a fowl roasted over the coals. To a beginner, getting the bird secure may seem an exasperating task but is really a simple procedure once one knows how.

To prepare the bird for the spit, salt the cavity and fold skin at top back over the neck, then fold under. Secure the skin by sewing with a needle and heavy thread or by poking a short skewer through the skin and tying the skin in place with string.

To secure to spit, attach holding fork on rod and push to back. Insert spit rod through center of bird; pinch fork tines together and push into the breast. With heavy string, tie wings against breast. Cross legs and tie to rod, looping string around the tail; knot securely. With another piece of string, tie the string around legs and around wings to further secure the bird.

Several small birds can be secured on one spit in the same way. When securing a turkey to the spit, it is important to insert the spit directly through the center yet angling downward to avoid the breastbone. Secure turkey wings and legs with extra-heavy cord to prevent them from burning.

ALMOND CHICKEN

¾ to 1 lb. cut-up chicken per person
1 t. each celery salt, onion salt, paprika, nutmeg, cinnamon
¼ t. ginger
2 T. almond extract

Wash chicken thoroughly; dry. Prick skin and meat. Place in shallow baking dish. Sprinkle with seasoning; cover tightly. Let rest at room temperature 2 hours.

Briquet Covered Cooking, Flat Grill or Gas Method: Barbecue over medium indirect heat for 1½ to 2 hours or until golden brown and tender.

CHICKEN CACCIATORE

¾ to 1 lb. cut-up chicken per person
Italian Sauce, p. 53
1 3-oz. can tomato paste
2 to 3 cans water
2 c. thinly sliced mushrooms

Wash chicken thoroughly; dry. Prick skin. Marinate 1 hour in Italian Sauce. Remove from sauce and refrigerate overnight. Add tomato paste and water to Italian Sauce to thicken; heat.

Briquet Covered Cooking and Gas Method: Barbecue over medium indirect heat. Place chicken skin side down. Turn frequently. Barbecue 1½ hours. Baste frequently with warm sauce. Place chicken in baking dish with sauce; add mushrooms. Spoon sauce over chicken. Return to grill; barbecue 1 hour longer.

BARBECUED CHICKEN BREASTS

2 T. chopped onion
1 T. butter
1 c. catsup
½ c. water
¼ c. brown sugar
3 T. vinegar
2 T. Worcestershire sauce
1 t. dry mustard
8 chicken breasts

Sauté onion in butter until golden. Add remaining ingredients, except chicken, and simmer 15 minutes. Serves 4 to 6.

Briquet Covered Cooking or Gas Method: Place chicken breasts, flesh side up, on grill. Barbecue over low indirect heat 15 minutes, brushing frequently with sauce. Turn chicken and barbecue another 15 minutes, basting with sauce. Serve with additional sauce.

LEMON BARBECUED CHICKEN

½ **cut-up chicken per person**
  Lemon Sauce, p. 53

Place chicken in Lemon Sauce and allow to stand 30 minutes. Barbecue over direct heat. Turn and baste often with the sauce. Cook until tender or fork turns easily in the meat.

CHICKEN AND RICE

  1 **c. uncooked rice**
2½ **c. water**
  2 **tomatoes, peeled and chopped**
  1 **small onion, finely chopped**
  ½ **lb. fresh mushrooms, sliced**
  ½ **c. chopped green pepper**
  2 **lbs. cut-up chicken**

Combine all ingredients except chicken; pour in a 9 x 12-inch aluminum foil pan. Lay chicken pieces on top. Serves 4.

Briquet Covered Cooking Method: Barbecue over low heat 2 hours; remove foil last 30 minutes.

CHICKEN BREASTS WITH ORANGE SAUCE

1 **to 2 chicken breasts per person**
  Salt, pepper, and paprika
  Orange Sauce, p. 54

Combine salt, pepper, and paprika in a shaker bag. Wash chicken breasts thoroughly; dry. Place breasts in shaker bag, one at a time and coat completely. Shake off excess. Chill for at least 1 hour.

Briquet Covered Cooking Method: Barbecue over medium direct heat. Place breasts skin side down. Barbecue 1½ hours. Turn frequently. Baste with Orange Sauce every 7 to 10 minutes the last 40 minutes of barbecuing time.

Gas Method: Barbecue over medium/low direct heat. Place breasts skin side down. Barbecue 1½ to 2 hours. Turn frequently. Baste with Orange Sauce every 10 minutes the last 40 to 50 minutes of barbecuing time.

Photograph opposite:
Chicken Breasts with Orange Sauce

BARBECUED CHICKEN

Purchase broiler fryers, allowing a half or quarter chicken per person. Rinse, pat dry and sprinkle with salt and pepper to taste.

Briquet Covered Cooking Method: Place chicken skin side up on grate about 5 inches above medium heat. Broil slowly for 10 to 15 minutes, then turn and broil skin side down until brown. Turn several times more and begin to baste about 10 minutes before chicken is done; barbecue sauce burns easily. Allow about 45 minutes total time for chickens weighing 1½ pounds, 1 to 1¼ hours for 2 to 2¼-pound chickens. Chicken is done when the drumstick can be twisted easily. Spoon the remaining barbecue sauce over chicken when serving.

SPICED CHICKEN

¾ **to 1 lb. cut-up chicken per person**
  ½ **t. onion salt**
  ½ **t. garlic salt**
  1 **t. ginger**
  ½ **t. cinnamon**
  ¼ **t. allspice**
  ¼ **t. powdered anise seed**
  ¼ **t. ground cloves**
  1 **t. salt**
  1 **T. monosodium glutamate**
  ⅛ **t. pepper**

Combine spices in mortar. Powder well with pestle. Wash chicken thoroughly; dry. Sprinkle spice mixture over entire surface of chicken. Refrigerate at least 1 hour.

Briquet Cooking, Flat Grill or Gas Method: Barbecue over medium indirect heat. Place chicken skin side down on grill. Barbecue 1½ to 2 hours or until tender. Turn frequently. Sprinkle with remaining spice mixture while barbecuing.

CHICKEN PACKETS

1 broiler fryer, quartered
1 envelope dehydrated onion soup
4 T. butter
1 t. paprika
1 4-oz. can mushrooms, drained
½ c. cream

Rinse chicken, dry, and remove small protruding bones. Cut 4 squares heavy-duty aluminum foil. On each square put 1 teaspoon butter, 1 tablespoon soup mix, and ¼ teaspoon paprika. Add one quarter of the chicken. Sprinkle with remaining soup. Add mushrooms and cream to each serving. Bring foil up over the food, sealing edges with a tight double fold.

Briquet Covered Cooking or Gas Method: Barbecue Chicken Packets on hot grill until tender, about 45 minutes to 1 hour. Turn chicken every 10 minutes.

CURRIED CHICKEN

½ c. melted butter
½ t. curry powder
1 2 to 2½-lb. chicken, cut up

Stir curry powder into melted butter. Serves 4.

Briquet Covered Cooking Method or Gas Method: Barbecue over low direct heat for 1½ to 2 hours, turning chicken frequently and basting with curry-butter.

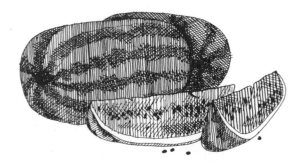

ROLLED TURKEY ROAST

¼ c. melted butter
1 clove garlic, minced
½ t. rosemary
1 4 to 5-lb. frozen rolled, boneless turkey roast, thawed

Combine butter, garlic, and rosemary. Secure turkey roast on spit. Place a foil pan below roast to catch drippings. Serves 8.

Spit Method: Barbecue roast on a rotating spit for 2 to 2½ hours or until meat thermometer register 190°. Baste with seasoned butter the last 30 minutes of cooking.

SQUABS

1 squab per person
Salt and pepper
Melted butter
Plum Sauce, p. 54

Wash squabs thoroughly; dry. Salt and pepper entire surface.

Briquet Covered Cooking or Gas Method: Barbecue over high indirect heat. Place squabs, breast side down. Turn and brush with melted butter frequently. Baste with Plum Sauce every 10 minutes the last half hour of barbecuing. Total barbecuing time: 45 minutes to 1 hour.

Spit Method: Secure birds on spit tightly. Barbecue over high indirect heat for 1 to 1¼ hours. Brush frequently with melted butter. Baste with Plum Sauce every 10 minutes the last half hour of barbecuing time.

TURKEY

1 turkey drumstick or thigh per person
Salt and pepper

Wash turkey thoroughly; dry. Sprinkle with salt and pepper.

Briquet Covered Cooking, Flat Grill or Gas Method: Barbecue over medium indirect heat for 2½ to 3 hours or until meat is very tender.

TURKEY FRUIT BOWL

1 15-lb. turkey
Salt
2 bananas (sliced in 2-inch segments)
1 small can peaches (drained and dried)
Fruit Compote, p. 33

Wash turkey thoroughly. Remove all fat from inside cavity. Salt entire bird.

Briquet Covered Cooking or Gas Method: Barbecue over medium indirect heat for 2½ to 3 hours. Place skin side down. Turn frequently. Add peaches and bananas to Fruit Compote. Fill turkey cavity with Fruit Compote last half hour of cooking time. Serves 8 to 12.

STUFFED TURKEY THIGHS

1 turkey thigh per person
¼ to ½ c. Sweet Sour Stuffing, p. 48
Salt and pepper

Remove thigh bone from meat and increase pocket size. Wash meat thoroughly; dry. Salt and pepper pocket. Fill pocket with stuffing. Secure tightly with skewers or string wrappings. Salt outside of stuffed thighs.

Briquet Covered Cooking, Flat Grill, or Gas Method: Barbecue over medium indirect heat for 2 hours or until meat is tender.

Spit Method: Place stuffed thighs in flat barbecue basket. Secure top tightly. Barbecue over medium heat for 2½ hours or until meat is tender.

TURKEY AND BACON

1 turkey thigh per person
2 slices Canadian bacon per turkey thigh
2 slices bacon per turkey thigh

Remove skin and bone from turkey thigh. Slice inside pocket back to edge of thigh, but do not go through thigh edges. Wash turkey thoroughly. Dry. Lay flat. Place Canadian bacon on turkey meat. Roll up. Roll bacon strips around outside of turkey roll; secure with skewers or toothpicks.

Briquet Covered Cooking, Flat Grill or Gas Method: Barbecue over medium indirect heat for 1½ to 2 hours or until meat is tender.

Spit Method: Place in flat barbecue basket. Barbecue over medium indirect heat for 2 hours or until meat is tender.

ITALIAN TURKEY BREASTS

1 3½ to 5-lb. turkey breast
Salt, pepper, paprika
Italian Sauce, p. 53
Melted butter

Wash breast thoroughly. Dry. Marinate in Italian Sauce overnight. Remove and dry. Sprinkle with salt, pepper, and paprika. Serves 2 to 3.

Briquet Covered Cooking or Gas Method: Barbecue over medium indirect heat for 2 hours. Place skin side down. Turn occasionally. Brush with melted butter while barbecuing.

ROAST TURKEY ON A SPIT

Rub inside cavity with salt. Secure bird to spit, checking balance. Place foil pan under bird to catch drippings. Brush bird with vegetable oil while roasting.

Spit Method: Barbecue over low heat 15 minutes per pound or until thermometer inserted in thigh registers 195°. Check turkey about 15 minutes before it should be done by snipping cord around drumsticks and moving drumstick. If it moves easily, bird is done.

ROYAL DUCK BREASTS

1 duck breast per person
½ lb. butter or margarine
1 c. sherry
1 T. currant jelly
1 T. Worcestershire sauce

Combine butter, sherry, jelly, and Worcestershire sauce in pan. Bring to a boil. Prick duck breasts and marinate in sauce for 1 hour. Place on barbecue (cut side down) with low heat. Barbecue 15 to 20 minutes. Turn frequently during barbecuing. Brush with sauce last 10 minutes. Serve with sauce.

ROAST DUCKLING WITH HONEY GLAZE

1 lb. duckling per person
Salt
1 c. honey
½ t. crushed celery seed or salt
1 t. brown sugar
Water

Wash duckling thoroughly; dry. Prick skin and meat with sharp fork. Salt inside cavity. Secure legs, wings and tail securely. Salt entire outside of bird. Combine honey, crushed celery seed, brown sugar and enough water to make medium consistency glaze.

Briquet Covered Cooking Method: Barbecue over medium indirect heat. Place breast side down. Barbecue 30 to 40 minutes. Turn bird, barbecue 2 hours. Allow coals to cool slightly. Brush with honey glaze every 15 minutes the last hour of barbecuing. Total barbecuing time: 2½ to 2¾ hours.

Gas Method: Barbecue over medium indirect heat. Place breast side down. Barbecue 30 to 45 minutes. Turn bird. Barbecue 1 hour. Reduce heat to low. Brush with honey glaze every 15 minutes, continue barbecuing 1 hour. Total barbecuing time: 2½ to 2¾ hours.

Spit Method: Place duckling on spit securely. Barbecue over medium indirect heat for 2½ hours. Brush with honey glaze every 15 minutes the last hour of barbecuing.

ROAST DUCKLING

1 3½-lb. duckling
Salt and pepper

Rub inside cavity of duck with salt. Prick skin with a fork. Secure duckling to spit and tie securely. Attach spit and place a foil pan under bird to catch drippings. Serves 4.

Briquet Covered Cooking or Gas Method: Barbecue over medium indirect heat about 2½ hours or until internal temperature registers 190°. Pour drippings from pan occasionally to prevent a fire.

ROCK CORNISH GAME HENS

1 hen per person
Salt and pepper
Melted butter

Wash hens thoroughly; dry. Salt and pepper.

Briquet Covered Cooking or Gas Method: Barbecue on medium indirect heat for 1 to 1½ hours. Baste frequently with melted butter.

Spit Method: Place securely on spit. Barbecue over medium indirect heat for 1½ to 1¾ hours. Baste frequently with melted butter.

GOOSE WITH FRUIT

1 lb. goose per person
Fruit Compote, p. 33
Salt

Wash goose thoroughly. Remove all excess fat. Dry. Prick skin and meat over entire surface. Stuff cavities with Fruit Compote. Secure tightly. Place extra skewers in meaty areas (legs, thighs, and breasts).

Spit Method: Place goose on spit securely. Barbecue over medium indirect heat for 3 to 4 hours or until golden brown and tender.

Fish

FILLET OF SOLE

½ lb. fillet of sole per person
Butter
Lemon juice
Salt
White pepper
Paprika

Wash fillet thoroughly. Place each fillet on well buttered aluminum foil. Sprinkle with lemon juice, salt, white pepper, and paprika. Wrap, securing ends. Barbecue over medium heat 15 to 20 minutes.

CRAB CAKES

2 c. crab meat
1 t. salt
¼ t. pepper
1 c. finely blended bread crumbs
2 eggs
2 T. Worcestershire sauce

Combine all ingredients. Mix well. Form into 4 to 6 patties. Wrap each patty in well-greased aluminum foil. Barbecue over medium direct heat for 10 to 15 minutes. Makes 4 to 6 cakes.

CRAB BOATS

2 c. crab meat
¾ c. finely sliced celery
1 T. snipped parsley
½ c. finely chopped mushrooms
3 T. finely chopped onion
3 t. finely chopped pimiento
1 T. prepared mustard
½ c. finely blended bread crumbs
1 egg
Salt and pepper to taste
Evaporated milk

Mix all ingredients with enough evaporated milk to moisten. Divide and pat into 6 to 8 aluminum foil boats. Barbecue over medium direct heat for 20 to 25 minutes. Makes 4 to 5 servings.

WARMED OYSTERS

6 to 8 oysters per person
1 lemon

Have oysters opened at market. Place oysters in deeper half shell in aluminum foil pan. Cut lemon in half. Add a few drops of lemon juice to each oyster. Add small amount of water to bottom of pan. Cover with aluminum foil. Barbecue over low direct heat for 15 to 20 minutes.

SCALLOPS

⅓ to ¼ lb. scallops per person
White Wine Marinade, p. 56
Melted butter

Marinate scallops in White Wine Marinade for 2 hours. Remove; chill thoroughly. Thread on skewers. Barbecue over medium direct heat until golden brown. Turn frequently and baste with White Wine Marinade and melted butter.

TROUT

1 trout per person
½ c. white wine
½ c. melted butter
1 t. salt
Dash of pepper
1 T. chopped fresh parsley per trout
½ thinly sliced lemon per trout
6 to 8 thin onion slices per trout

Wash fish thoroughly; dry. Mix white wine, melted butter, salt, and pepper. Brush fish cavity with wine butter. Sprinkle cavity with chopped parsley. Lay lemon and onion slices in fish cavity. Secure with toothpicks or lace tightly. Brush entire surface of trout with wine butter.

Briquet Covered Cooking, Flat Grill or Gas Method: Barbecue over medium direct heat until brown. Turn once. Allow 15 to 20 minutes total barbecuing time.

SHRIMP KEBABS

1 lb. green shrimp
1 1-lb. can pineapple chunks
¼ c. soy sauce
4 slices bacon, cut in 2-inch squares

Combine shrimp, pineapple chunks, and soy sauce in a bowl. Set aside for 30 minutes. Alternate shrimp, pineapple, and bacon on short skewers. Place each skewer in the center of a lightly greased square of aluminum foil. Fold edges together, securing well. Serves about 4.

Briquet Covered Cooking Method: Barbecue over medium heat for about 12 to 15 minutes, turning once.

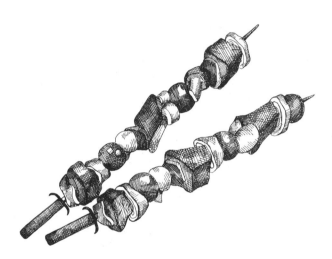

SAVORY OUTDOOR BAKED FISH

Scale and clean fish, leaving whole or cut into fillets or steaks. Place fish on individual sheets of heavy-duty foil and brush with oil or melted butter. Sprinkle with salt, pepper, and lemon juice. Top each fish with a teaspoonful of chopped tomato or pimiento, garnish with lemon slices. Bring foil up over fish and seal with a double fold. Seal ends.

Briquet Covered Cooking Method: Place on grate over a medium-high fire and bake 10 minutes per side for a small 1 to 1½-pound fish, 15 minutes on a side for 2 to 3-pound fish and about 20 minutes on a side for a 4 to 5-pound fish. Open foil and test with a fork. Fish is done when it flakes easily. Also serve the juice from the package.

FISH BANQUET

1 1-lb. fish
2 slices bacon
2 potatoes, peeled and sliced
1 onion, sliced
Salt and pepper to taste

Cut off a 12-inch square of aluminum foil. Lay 1 slice of bacon in foil. Place the fish on top of bacon. Top with second bacon slice. Add potatoes and onion. Season to taste. Wrap food in foil, folding edges and ends over twice. Place upside down on another piece of foil. Seal again.

Briquet Covered Cooking Method: Place packet in hot ashes or on top of grill away from direct flame. Cook 15 to 20 minutes on each side after packet begins to sizzle. Remove the outer foil and serve.

SHRIMP SCAMPI

2 lbs. uncooked large shrimp
   (15 to 20 to a pound)
2 cloves garlic
¾ c. butter or margarine
½ t. each: tarragon, rosemary, thyme
3 T. lemon juice
1½ t. salt
Freshly ground pepper to taste

Remove shell, leaving tail in place and devein shrimp. Mince or crush the garlic and combine with butter or margarine and herbs in a small saucepan. Let stand over heat for a few minutes to blend flavors, then add lemon juice. Tear six 12-inch squares of heavy-duty aluminum foil and arrange 4 or 5 shrimp on each. Pour the garlic-butter mixture over and sprinkle each serving with salt and freshly ground pepper. Bring foil up over shrimp, gathering edges together and twist at top to form a poke. Barbecue as directed. Wrap French bread in foil and heat on the grill for 5 minutes, turning once. Serves 6.

Briquet Covered Cooking Method: Barbecue over a medium-high fire for 10 to 20 minutes.

SEAFOOD KEBABS

2 strips of bacon per person
¼ green pepper per person
⅓ lb. scallops per person
⅓ lb. cleaned raw shrimp per person
5 to 6 mushrooms per person
Melted butter

Cut bacon and green pepper in 1-inch squares. Thread ingredients alternately on long skewers. Barbecue over medium direct heat until golden brown. Turn frequently and brush with melted butter.

FISH STEAK

1 1-inch fish steak per person
Juice of half of one lemon
2 T. melted butter
Salt, pepper, and paprika to taste

Mix lemon juice and melted butter together.

Briquet Covered Cooking, Flat Grill, or Gas Method: Barbecue fish steak over medium direct heat. Allow 10 to 15 minutes total barbecuing time. Brush frequently with lemon butter. Turn once. Brush both sides of fish steaks with lemon butter. Sprinkle with salt, pepper, and paprika to serve.

LOBSTER KEBABS

½ to ¾ lb. lobster per person
1 small green pepper per person
5 to 6 cherry tomatoes per person
5 to 6 small white onions or shallots
½ c. melted butter
½ c. very dry sherry
Salt

Cut lobster and green peppers in 1-inch cubes. Thread lobster, tomatoes, onions, and peppers on skewers. Combine melted butter and salt to taste. Brush with melted butter, then sherry.

Briquet Covered Cooking, Flat Grill or Gas Method: Barbecue over medium direct heat until tender. Baste often with butter and sherry. Turn frequently. Allow 10 to 15 minutes total barbecuing time.

STUFFED FISH

1 whole fish with backbone removed
Celery Stuffing, p. 48
½ c. melted butter

Combine Celery Stuffing and 3 tablespoons melted butter. Wash fish thoroughly; dry. Fill cavity with Celery Stuffing. Lace to secure cavity. Baste fish completely with remaining melted butter. Barbecue over medium direct heat for 1 to 1½ hours. Baste fish with melted butter frequently. Turn occasionally to prevent sticking. Makes 3 to 5 servings.

PERCH KEBABS

2 lbs. perch fillets
½ c. vegetable oil
¼ c. lemon juice
1 t. salt
1 clove garlic, minced
¼ t. thyme
½ t. oregano
12 cherry tomatoes
12 small onions
12 green pepper chunks

Cut fish into 1-inch squares. Combine oil, lemon juice, spices, and garlic. Pour marinade over fish and let marinate 2 to 3 hours. Parboil onions and green peppers. On 6 skewers, alternate fish, tomatoes, onions, and green pepper. Serves 6.

Briquet Covered Cooking or Gas Method: Barbecue over medium heat 8 to 10 minutes, basting frequently.

FROG LEGS

3 to 4 frog legs per person
White Wine Marinade, p. 56
Salt and pepper
Melted butter

Cut frog legs in half at joint. Marinate in White Wine Marinade 1 to 2 hours. Remove from marinade and dry. Salt and pepper.

Briquet Covered Cooking, Flat Grill or Gas Method: Barbecue over medium direct heat until golden brown. Brush with melted butter and Wine Marinade.

Photograph opposite:
Lobster Kebabs

22

Lamb

LAMB

½ lb. lamb per person
1 lemon (cut in wedges)
Salt and pepper
Plum Sauce, p. 54

Wipe lamb off thoroughly with a damp cloth. Rub well with lemon. Salt and pepper to taste.

Briquet Covered Cooking Method: Barbecue over indirect heat for 2½ to 3 hours. (Add briquets as needed.) Brush with Plum Barbecue Sauce every 15 minutes the last hour of cooking.

Gas Method: Barbecue over indirect high heat for 1 hour. Turn heat to medium and finish cooking 1½ to 2 hours. Brush with Plum Barbecue Sauce every 15 minutes the last hour of cooking.

PROVINCIAL LAMB

Leg of lamb (¾ lb. per person)
1 c. dry white wine
1 lemon
3 t. garlic powder
1 t. rosemary
½ t. salt
Dash of pepper

Combine garlic powder, rosemary, salt, and pepper in mortar. Grind to a powder with pestle. Wash lamb thoroughly under cold running water. Dry. Rub with lemon peel. Puncture with ice pick at intervals and insert garlic mixture. Combine wine and juice from lemon.

Briquet Covered Cooking Method: Barbecue over medium indirect heat for 3 to 4 hours or until golden brown. Baste with wine mixture every ½ hour.

Gas Method: Barbecue over medium indirect heat for 3 to 4 hours or until golden brown. Baste with wine mixture every ½ hour.

SHISH KEBAB

¾ lb. lamb, per person
White Wine Marinade, p. 56

Cut lamb into 1-inch cubes. Marinate lamb in White Wine Marinade for 5 hours or overnight. Thread on skewers.

Briquet Covered Cooking, Flat Grill or Gas Method: Barbecue over high direct heat until crispy and brown on all sides.

LAMB STEW

1½ to 2 lbs. lamb chunks
4 c. potato chunks
2 c. onion chunks
2 c. carrot chunks
2 bay leaves
2 T. butter or margarine
Salt and pepper

Salt and pepper lamb chunks completely. Place all ingredients in baking dish. Add 2 to 3 cups water. Salt and pepper entire mixture. Makes 5 to 6 servings.

Briquet Covered Cooking or Gas Method: Barbecue over medium indirect heat for 2½ to 3 hours or until meat is tender. Remove bay leaves and thicken gravy.

EASTER CROWN LAMB

1 crown lamb roast (¾ lb. per person)
Salt and pepper
Sweet Stuffing, p. 48

Place lamb on shallow aluminum foil pan. Season completely. Fill crown with Sweet Stuffing. Edge around bone tips with aluminum foil (shiny side out).

Briquet Covered Cooking Method: Barbecue over indirect heat. Allow 15 minutes per pound.

Gas Method: Barbecue over medium indirect heat. Allow 15 minutes per pound.

ROLLED LAMB SHOULDER

½ lb. rolled lamb shoulder per person
1 t. celery salt
2 t. onion salt
½ t. lemon pepper

Combine salts and pepper. Season lamb thoroughly.

Briquet Covered Cooking Method: Barbecue over medium indirect heat 3 to 3½ hours or until fork tender.

Gas and Spit Method: Barbecue over medium indirect heat 3 to 4 hours or until fork tender.

STUFFED BREAST OF LAMB

1 lamb breast (¾ lb. per person)
Salt and pepper
Celery Dressing, p. 48

Cut pocket in lamb breast. Season with salt and pepper. Fill cavity with Celery Dressing. Secure tightly with thread or skewers. Season outside of breast.

Briquet Covered Cooking Method: Barbecue over medium indirect heat for 2½ to 3 hours.

Gas Method: Barbecue over medium indirect heat for 1½ to 3 hours.

LAMB CURRY

2 lbs. lamb cut in 1-inch cubes
1 t. curry powder
1½ t. salt
4 to 8 large apples, sliced
Acorn squash cut in 1-inch cubes
Curry Sauce, p. 53

Place curry powder and salt in a shaker bag. Add lamb and shake until completely coated. Thread meat alternately with apples and squash on skewers. Serves 4.

Briquet Covered Cooking, Flat Grill or Gas Method: Barbecue over medium direct heat for 40 to 45 minutes or until lamb is crispy and browned. Baste with Curry Sauce once at end of barbecue. Serve over rice with hot Curry Sauce.

LAMB SHANKS

1 shank per person
3 T. herb seasoning
1 T. dried lemon peel

Combine herb seasoning and lemon peel. Season each shank thoroughly, rubbing seasoning into surface of shank with heel of your hand.

Briquet Covered Cooking Method: Barbecue over medium indirect heat for 2½ to 3 hours.

Gas Method: Barbecue over medium/low indirect heat for 2½ to 3 hours.

LAMB STEAKETTES

2 lamb steakettes per person
Lemon Marinade, p. 53 *or*
Soy Marinade, p. 56

Place steakettes in marinade and refrigerate overnight.

Briquet Covered Cooking, Flat Grill or Gas Method: Barbecue over high direct heat. Allow 12 to 14 minutes total barbecuing time.

LAMB CHOP MADEIRA

2 lamb chops per person
⅛ c. butter or margarine
1 small bay leaf
Pinch of thyme
1 c. Madeira

Melt butter. Add bay leaf and thyme. Cook over very low heat 2 to 3 minutes. Remove from heat. Add Madeira. Mix well. Place lamb chops in shallow baking dish. Pour over Madeira sauce. Allow to rest 1 hour.

Briquet Covered Cooking Method: Barbecue over medium indirect heat for 20 minutes or until golden brown.

Gas Method: Barbecue over medium indirect heat for 20 minutes or until golden brown.

Pork

PORK ROAST

½ lb. pork roast per person
Salt and pepper or
Barbecue Sauce I or II, p. 53

Rinse roast under cold water. Season with salt and pepper or baste with barbecue sauce.

Briquet covered cooking method: Barbecue over indirect heat for 2¼ or 3 hours. Add briquets as needed. No turning necessary.

Gas method: Barbecue over indirect high heat for 1 hour. Turn heat to medium and finish cooking 1½ to 2 hours.

HAWAIIAN PORK STEAK

1 large pork steak per person
1 4-oz. can pineapple chunks
½ sweet potato per person
1 T. brown sugar per serving
½ strip of bacon per serving

Place pork steak, pineapple chunks, sweet potato, and brown sugar in a square of aluminum foil. Top with ½ strip of bacon. Wrap securely.

Briquet Covered Cooking, Flat Grill, and Gas Method: Barbecue over medium direct heat for 1 hour.

PORK TENDERLOIN

Pork tenderloin (½ lb. per person)
4 to 6 slices bacon

Arrange bacon on top of tenderloin. Secure with toothpicks.

Briquet Covered Cooking Method: Barbecue over medium indirect heat until tender. Allow 25 to 30 minutes per pound. May be brushed with favorite barbecue sauce.

Gas Method: Barbecue over medium indirect heat until tender. Allow 20 to 25 minutes per pound. May be brushed with favorite barbecue sauce.

PORK LUNCHEON STEAKS

2 pork luncheon steaks per person
Salt and pepper to taste

Season pork steaks with salt and pepper.

Briquet Covered Cooking, Flat Grill or Gas Method: Barbecue over medium direct heat. Allow 17 to 20 minutes total barbecuing time.

STUFFED PORK CHOPS

1 double pork chop per person
Sweet Stuffing, p. 48
Sweet Sauce, p. 54

Cut pocket into pork chops. Fill with Sweet Stuffing. Secure tightly.

Briquet Covered Cooking, Flat Grill or Gas Method: Barbecue over medium direct heat for 45 minutes. Turn once. Brush with Sweet Sauce every 15 minutes.

CROWN PORK ROAST

1 crown pork roast (¾ to 1 lb. per person)
Salt and pepper
Sweet Sour Stuffing, p. 48

Season roast with salt and pepper. Place aluminum foil on end of bones securely (shiny side out).

Briquet Covered Cooking Method: Barbecue over medium indirect heat. Place roast on rib rack, bone side down. Barbecue 1 hour. Remove. Place roast in aluminum foil pan. Fill crown with Sweet Sour Stuffing. Barbecue 2 to 2½ hours or until meat is tender.

Gas Method: Barbecue over low indirect heat. Place roast on grill, bone side down. Barbecue 1 hour. (Watch for flame-ups). Remove. Place roast in aluminum foil pan. Fill crown with Sweet Sour Stuffing. Barbecue over medium indirect heat for 2½ to 3 hours or until meat is tender.

Photograph opposite:
Lamb Chop Madeira, p. 25

PORK SAUSAGES OR BRATWURST

2 to 3 sausages per person

Prick each sausage several times.

Briquet Covered Cooking, Flat Grill, or Gas Method: Barbecue over medium direct heat. Turn frequently. (Watch for flame-ups.) Allow 15 to 20 minutes total barbecuing time.

BACON AND EGGS

1 or 2 eggs per person
2 to 3 slices of bacon per person
Salt and pepper

Place eggs in a dish. Add salt and pepper to taste. Mix well. Place in a greased aluminum foil pan.

Briquet Covered Cooking Method: Barbecue over direct medium heat. Lay bacon strips on grill surface. Place pan of eggs over heat; stir occasionally. Allow 10 to 15 minutes total barbecuing time.

Gas Method: Barbecue over low direct heat. Place bacon strips on grill surface. Place pan of eggs over heat; stir occasionally. Allow 10 to 15 minutes total barbecuing time.

WESTERN HAM

5 to 10-lb. country ham (with bone)
10 to 12 whole cloves
1 12-oz. can pineapple slices
6 to 8 maraschino cherries
Pineapple Glaze, p. 56

With a sharp knife, remove as much skin and fat as possible from ham. Puncture at intervals with an ice pick and insert whole cloves. Serves about 6 to 12.

Briquet Covered Cooking and Gas Method: Barbecue ham over medium indirect heat for 2½ to 3 hours. Baste with Pineapple Glaze every 15 minutes the last hour of cooking. Remove cloves. Place pineapple slices with cherry centers on top of ham. Secure with toothpicks. Baste once. Close cover and barbecue for 20 minutes.

HAM HOCKS AND KRAUT

1 smoked ham hock per person
1 c. of sauerkraut per person
1 medium onion (chopped)
1 T. sugar
¼ t. caraway seed

Mix sauerkraut, onion, sugar, and caraway seed. Grease inside of foil tray. Place kraut mixture on bottom. Top with smoked ham hocks.

Briquet Covered Cooking Method: Cover and barbecue over indirect heat for 2 hours.

Gas Method: Cover and barbecue over indirect medium heat, 2 hours.

HCBT SANDWICH

1 slice ham per sandwich
1 slice cheese per sandwich
1 slice bacon per sandwich
1 slice tomato per sandwich
1 English muffin per sandwich

Briquet Covered Cooking, Flat Grill or Gas Method: Barbecue ham and bacon over medium direct heat. Toast English muffin on grill top. Place cheese on ham. Allow to slightly melt. Place bacon on top of cheese. Place ham, cheese, and bacon on half of English muffin. Top with tomato slice and other half of muffin.

HAM AND CHEESE KEBABS

8 thin slices boiled ham
24 ½-inch cubes American cheese
Prepared mustard

Cut ham slices into 1-inch strips; spread with mustard. Wrap ham slice around cube of cheese. Place on thin skewers. Serves 8.

Briquet Covered Cooking Method: Rotate skewer over medium coals for 2 or 3 minutes until cheese begins to melt.

PORK LOAF

2 lbs. pork sausage
2 c. crushed potato chips
1 10½-oz. can cream of mushroom soup
½ can water
1 small onion, chopped
1 T. chopped parsley
  Salt and pepper

Combine all ingredients thoroughly. Place in an ungreased aluminum foil pan. Makes 4 to 6 servings.

Briquet Covered Cooking Method: Barbecue over medium indirect heat for 1½ to 2 hours.

Gas Method: Barbecue over medium indirect heat for 1½ to 2 hours.

MUSTARD HAM SLICE

1 ham slice per person
  Sweet Mustard Sauce, p. 53
¼ c. milk

Thin Mustard Sauce with milk. Baste one side of ham slice.

Briquet Covered Cooking Method: Place mustard side down. Barbecue over medium direct heat 5 to 7 minutes. Baste top side of ham slice. Turn. Barbecue 5 to 7 minutes.

Gas Method: Place mustard side down. Barbecue over medium/low heat 5 to 7 minutes. Baste top side of ham slice. Turn. Barbecue 5 to 7 minutes.

LIVER AND BACON ROLL-UPS

2 slices liver per person
2 to 3 slices bacon per person
  Salt and pepper

Slice liver the width of bacon. Lay liver strip on top of bacon strip. Salt and pepper to taste. Roll jelly-roll style; secure with toothpick.

Flat-top grill method: Place Roll-Ups on grill and barbecue 2 to 3 inches above briquets. Turn several times to brown evenly. Allow 20 to 25 minutes total barbecuing time.

Spit Method: Place in flat spit basket. Barbecue over indirect heat for 30 to 35 minutes.

BACON WRAPPED WEINERS

1 strip bacon per weiner
1 weiner

Wrap bacon around weiner. Secure with skewer or toothpicks. Barbecue over medium heat until bacon is cooked. Turn frequently.

ITALIAN FRANKS

2 to 3 weiners per person
  Italian Marinade, p. 53

Prick skins of weiners. Marinate weiners in Italian Marinade overnight. Barbecue over medium heat for 10 minutes. Turn frequently.

RABBIT

⅓ rabbit, cleaned, per person
  White Wine Marinade, p. 56
  Salt and pepper

Wash and dry rabbit. Marinate in White Wine Marinade 1 to 2 hours. Remove and dry. Sprinkle with salt and pepper. Barbecue over medium indirect heat 1 to 1½ hours or until meat is tender.

VENISON ROAST

1 lb. of roast per person
  Soy, White or Red Wine Marinade, p. 56
  Salt and pepper
4 to 6 strips of bacon

Remove skin and tough sinews from meat. Wash thoroughly. Marinate in Soy, White or Red Wine Marinade 2 to 3 days. Turn frequently. Remove from marinade and dry. Sprinkle with salt and pepper. Wrap bacon strips around venison roast. Secure tightly with skewers or toothpicks.

Briquet Covered Cooking or Gas Method: Barbecue over high indirect heat. Allow 15 to 20 minutes per pound. Turn occasionally.

Veal

VEAL CHOPS

1 veal shoulder chop per person
White Wine Marinade, p. 56

Marinate chops in White Wine Marinade 2 to 3 hours. Remove and chill thoroughly. Barbecue over medium direct heat 10 minutes per side or until brown and tender.

VEAL CUTLET

2 to 3 veal cutlets per person
Sweet Mustard Sauce, p. 53
1 t. horseradish

Blend horseradish with Sweet Mustard Sauce. Barbecue over medium direct heat for 10 to 15 minutes. Spread sauce on each side of cutlet once.

VEAL ROMA

½ lb. veal round steak per person
1 3-oz. can tomato paste
3 cans water
1 t. garlic powder
2 t. oregano
1 t. salt
½ t. pepper
1 t. sugar
1 c. thinly sliced mushrooms
1 c. dry red wine
1 c. grated Mozzarella cheese

Cut veal steak into serving size pieces. Place steaks in well-greased aluminum foil pan. Combine tomato paste, water, garlic powder, oregano, salt, pepper, and sugar. Mix well. Add mushrooms and wine. Stir. Pour tomato mixture over veal steaks.

Briquet Covered Cooking or Gas Method: Barbecue over medium indirect heat for 1½ hours or until meat is tender. Garnish with Mozzarella cheese.

VEAL MINUTE STEAKS

2 veal minute steaks per person
Plum Glaze, p. 54

Briquet Covered Cooking, Flat Grill or Gas Method: Barbecue over medium direct heat for 12 to 15 minutes. Baste with Plum Glaze. Allow 12 to 15 minutes total barbecuing time.

VEAL STEAKS

1 veal steak per person
Salt and pepper

Briquet Covered Cooking Method: Barbecue over medium indirect heat. Season steaks and sear them directly over the coals. Then place them over drip pan and barbecue for 15 to 20 minutes or until tender. Turn once.

Gas Method: Season steaks and sear them over high direct heat. Reduce heat to low and barbecue for 15 to 20 minutes or until tender. Turn once.

STUFFED VEAL ROAST

½ to ¾ lb. boned veal rump roast per person
¼ to ½ c. Sweet Sour Stuffing, p. 48
½ lb. bacon

Fry bacon until translucent. Combine 2 tablespoons bacon drippings with Sweet Sour Dressing. Lay veal roast flat. Spread stuffing on roast. Roll tightly. Wrap veal roll with cooked bacon. Secure tightly with skewers or toothpicks. Secure entire roast with string.

Briquet Covered Cooking or Gas Method: Barbecue over medium indirect heat for 2 to 2½ hours. Turn occasionally.

Spit Method: Place roast on spit securely. Barbecue over medium heat 2½ to 3 hours.

Photograph opposite:
Veal Roma

Ribs

SPANISH SPARERIBS

¾ to 1 lb. pork spareribs per person
1 c. cider vinegar
1 c. dry white wine
1 T. ground cumin
2 T. garlic powder
¼ t. cayenne
1 t. lemon pepper
2 t. salt
Water

Combine vinegar, wine, cumin, garlic, cayenne, lemon pepper, salt, and enough water to cover spareribs. Marinate several days, turning occasionally. Remove from marinade and dry.

Briquet Covered Cooking, Flat Grill, or Gas Method: Barbecue over medium indirect heat for 1½ to 2 hours.

GLAZED CHINESE-STYLE SPARERIBS

4 to 5 lbs. spareribs
1½ t. salt
½ t. garlic salt
½ c. apple or currant jelly
⅓ c. pineapple juice
¼ c. honey
1 T. soy sauce
½ t. ginger
1 30-oz. can pineapple slices, drained

Cut ribs into 3 or 4-rib sections. Combine salts and rub over ribs. In a saucepan, combine jelly, juice, honey, soy sauce, and ginger. Simmer 5 minutes, stirring often. Serve with pineapple slices. Serves 6.

Briquet Covered Cooking or Gas Method: Barbecue, meaty side up, over low direct heat for 30 minutes. Turn meaty side down and barbecue 15 minutes; turn bone side down and barbecue another 30 minutes. Baste with sauce and barbecue an additional 30 minutes, basting frequently with sauce. Brush both sides with sauce just before serving.

LUAU RIBS

4 lbs. meaty spareribs, cut in narrow strips
¼ c. molasses
¼ c. soy sauce
¼ c. sugar
¾ c. vinegar
¾ c. pineapple juice

Combine molasses, soy sauce, sugar, vinegar, and pineapple juice. Heat, stirring, until sugar dissolves. Pour over ribs and marinate overnight. Lace ribs on spit accordion-style. Alternate ribs with pineapple chunks and green pepper cubes. Serves 4.

Spit Method: Barbecue on a rotating spit 1 hour or more, basting frequently with sauce.

COUNTRY RIBS AND KRAUT

4 lbs. country ribs, cut in 2-rib sections
1 lb. sauerkraut
2 apples

Core apples, slice in rings. Place kraut in a 9 x 12-inch aluminum pan. Arrange ribs on kraut, cover with apple slice. Serves 4.

Briquet Covered Cooking Method: Barbecue over medium coals 1½ to 2 hours.

RIBS AND ORANGE SAUCE

½ c. orange marmalade
¼ c. lemon juice
¼ c. soy sauce
1 clove garlic, minced
2 T. water
Salt and pepper
3 lbs. country-style pork ribs

In a saucepan, combine all ingredients except salt, pepper, and ribs. Simmer, stirring occasionally, for 15 minutes. Season ribs with salt and pepper. Place, bone side down, on grill. Serves 4.

Briquet Covered Cooking or Gas Method: Barbecue over medium direct heat 3 to 3½ hours. Baste with sauce the last 30 minutes of cooking.

Fruit

PEACH PERFECT

1 peach half per person
  Almond extract
  Nutmeg
  Sugar
1 maraschino cherry per peach half

Sprinkle peach half with almond extract, nutmeg, and sugar. Top with maraschino cherry. Wrap carefully in aluminum foil. Barbecue over medium indirect or direct heat for 7 to 10 minutes.

APPLE NUT

½ apple per person
¼ c. finely chopped walnuts
1 T. brown sugar
1 t. cinnamon
¼ t. nutmeg
2 T. ground sugared cereal flakes

Peel and slice apples. Combine apples, walnuts, sugar, cinnamon, and nutmeg. Mix well to coat. Place in well greased baking dish. Top with cereal flakes; cover. Barbecue over medium indirect heat for 20 to 30 minutes.

FRUIT COMPOTE

1 c. sliced celery
3 c. apple wedges
2 c. orange wedges
1 c. raisins
½ c. chopped walnuts
  Sprinkle of cinnamon

Combine all ingredients. Place in greased aluminum foil or use as stuffing. Barbecue over indirect or direct heat for 15 to 20 minutes. Makes 5½ cups.

BREAKFAST SUNSHINE

1 12-oz. can grapefruit and orange sections
1 t. sugar
  Dash of nutmeg

Remove paper label from fruit can. Drain sections slightly. Add sugar and dash of nutmeg to sections in can; stir gently. Cover with aluminum foil. Barbecue over medium heat 15 to 20 minutes. Makes 1½ cups.

SPICED PEARS

1 pear half per person
  Lemon juice
  Cinnamon
  Ginger

Sprinkle pear half with lemon juice, cinnamon, and ginger. Wrap carefully in aluminum foil. Barbecue over medium indirect/direct heat for 7 to 10 minutes.

TRIPLE TREAT

½ c. chopped cranberries
½ c. chopped apple
½ c. chopped pineapple
⅛ t. salt
½ c. sugar

Combine all ingredients. Mix well. Place in a small greased baking dish. Barbecue over medium indirect heat 30 minutes. Makes 1½ cups.

SOUTHERN RAISINS

¾ c. seeded raisins
1 c. sugar
1 t. lemon rind
1½ c. water
  Dash of salt

Combine all ingredients; mix well. Cover. Place in a well greased baking dish. Barbecue over low/medium indirect heat 50 to 60 minutes. Makes 1¼ cups.

Hors d'Oeuvres

MUSHROOMS

1 lb. medium mushrooms
¼ c. butter or margarine
2 T. chopped onion
2 T. soy sauce

Wash mushrooms; drain. Combine mushrooms, butter, onion, and soy sauce in a baking dish. Barbecue over medium heat until lightly browned. Stir or shake frequently. Serves 8 to 10.

HAM AND PINEAPPLE

2 c. cubed ham
1 8-oz. can pineapple chunks

Thread ham and pineapple chunks on skewers. Barbecue over medium heat 5 to 10 minutes. Turn frequently. Serves 8 to 10.

WEINER ROUNDS

1 pkg. weiners
Favorite barbecue sauce

Cut weiners into pennies. Place in a baking dish. Add barbecue sauce. Barbecue for 15 to 20 minutes. Serves 10 to 15.

TUNA CHEESE

1 12½-oz. can flaked tuna
1 8-oz. pkg. grated cheese
1 t. Worcestershire sauce
1 t. grated onion
Salad dressing
6 English muffins

Mix together tuna, cheese, Worcestershire sauce, onion, and enough salad dressing to moisten. Spread on English muffin half. Barbecue over medium heat until cheese slightly melts. Cut into fourths. Serves 10 to 12.

CHICKEN GIZZARDS

1 lb. chicken gizzards
Salt and pepper
Melted butter or margarine

Clean gizzards. Cut in half and remove tough center. Thread on skewers. Season with salt and pepper. Barbecue over medium heat for 15 to 20 minutes. Brush with melted butter. Turn frequently. Serves 8 to 10.

MARINATED CAULIFLOWER

1 head cauliflower
Italian Marinade, p. 53

Clean and divide cauliflower. Marinate in Italian Marinade 1 hour. Barbecue over medium heat 10 to 15 minutes. Serve hot. Serves 10 to 12.

SCALLOP WRAPS

1 lb. scallops
6 to 10 slices bacon

Wash scallops thoroughly; dry. Completely wrap each scallop with a piece of bacon. Thread on skewers. Barbecue over medium heat until golden brown. Turn frequently. Serves 8 t 10.

CRAB MUSHROOM

1 6½-oz. can crab meat (drained)
1 4-oz. can mushroom pieces (drained)
½ t. salt
Soft butter or margarine

Flake crab meat. Cut mushrooms into small pieces. Blend crab, mushrooms, and salt with enough soft butter to bind. Spread on crisp thins. Barbecue for 5 minutes. Serves 8 to 10.

Photograph opposite:
Crab Mushroom Hors d'Oeuvres

Backyard Burger Party

It's fun to celebrate any occasion with a cookout in your own backyard. You'll enjoy a real treat when your barbecue menu includes hamburgers. Here's a menu family and friends will like.

OREGANO DIP

1 t. oregano
½ t. grated onion
¼ t. salt
Few drops Tabasco
1 c. dairy sour cream

Blend all ingredients into sour cream. Cover and chill.

VEGETABLE DIPPERS

Use the following relishes with a favorite dip:

Radishes
Celery hearts
Cucumber slices
Carrot sticks
Cauliflowerets
Green onions
Broccoli buds
Cherry tomatoes

WATERMELON BASKET

½ watermelon
1 cantaloupe
1 qt. strawberries
1 qt. blueberries
1 qt. cherries
3 limes

Make large watermelon balls from half a watermelon, discarding seeds. Reserve the shell. Make smaller balls from cantaloupe. With a sharp knife, trim the edge of the watermelon shell by cutting a sawtooth edge. Fill shell with melon balls adding strawberries, blueberries, and cherries. Pile fruit high in the shell. Decorate with 3 quartered limes and a few mint leaves. Chill before serving.

STUFFED HAMBURGERS

1½ lbs. ground beef
1½ t. salt
1 c. packaged stuffing
1 medium onion, grated
¼ c. butter
2 T. lemon juice
¼ t. pepper

Mix ground beef and salt. Divide into 12 equal parts and flatten to about 5 inches in diameter. Combine remaining ingredients. Divide among 6 patties. Top each of the patties with stuffing mixture. Place remaining meat patties on top and press edges together with a fork. Barbecue over direct heat 20 minutes, turning once. Serves 6.

COOKOUT BURGERS

1½ lbs. ground beef
1 c. instant nonfat dry milk
1 t. salt
1 egg
1 T. instant minced onion

Combine all ingredients, mixing well. Shape into 6 patties. Barbecue over direct heat 10 minutes, turning once. Serves 4.

BEEF BURGERS

2 lbs. ground beef
½ c. finely chopped onion
2 t. salt
¼ t. pepper
2 eggs
Melted butter

Combine all ingredients, except melted butter, mixing well. Shape into 8 patties. Brush with melted butter and barbecue over direct heat 10 to 15 minutes, turning once. Serves 6.

HAWAIIN BURGERS

3 T. prepared mustard
3 T. catsup
1½ T. soy sauce
8 pineapple slices

Prepare Beef Burgers. Barbecue over direct heat for 10 to 15 minutes, basting with sauce. After turning burgers, top each with a pineapple slice.

GUACAMOLE-TOPPED BURGERS

1 avocado
½ c. chopped tomato
¼ c. chopped onion
1 T. lemon juice
¼ t. salt
¼ t. garlic salt
4 to 6 drops Tabasco
Dash pepper

Prepare Beef Burgers. Mash avocado; stir in remaining ingredients. Spoon avocado mixture onto sizzling hot Beef Burgers.

BROWNIES

2 c. sugar
⅓ c. cocoa
1 c. melted butter
4 eggs
2 t. vanilla
1½ c. sifted flour
1 t. salt
½ c. chopped nuts

Mix together sugar and cocoa. Stir in butter. Add eggs and vanilla and beat well. Sift together flour and salt and stir into cocoa mixture. Fold in nuts. Pour into a greased 15 x 10-inch jelly roll pan. Bake in a 375° oven 25 minutes. Cool and frost. Serves 8.

FROSTING

1 c. sugar
¼ c. butter
1 1-oz. square unsweetened chocolate
⅓ c. milk
Dash salt

Combine all ingredients in a saucepan. Bring to a boil, stirring constantly. Boil for 1 minute. Beat until of spreading consistency.

GEORGIA PEACH CAKE

1¼ c. sifted flour
¼ c. sugar
½ t. salt
1 t. baking powder
½ c. shortening
2 egg yolks, slightly beaten
2 T. milk

Stir dry ingredients together; cut in shortening as for a pie crust. Stir in egg yolks and milk, mixing with a fork. Press into the bottom of a 9 x 13-inch pan.

FILLING

4 large peaches, peeled and thinly sliced
¾ c. sugar
2 T. flour
2 T. butter
⅛ t. nutmeg

Place peach slices evenly over crust. Mix together remaining ingredients and sprinkle over peaches. Bake in a 350° oven for 50 minutes. Serves 8.

Casseroles

BRATS IN BEER AND BEANS

2 to 3 brats or pork sausage per person
Beer
1 1-lb. can pork and beans

Prick brats. Place in baking dish. Cover with beer. Open can of beans, leave in can.

Briquet Covered Cooking or Gas Method: Place brats in beer and can of beans, with top off, on grill. Barbecue over medium direct heat 30 to 40 minutes or until brats are cooked. Stir beans occasionally.

Flat Grill Method: Cover baking dish with aluminum foil. Place top on can of beans. Barbecue 30 to 40 minutes or until brats are cooked. Stir beans occasionally.

CHICKEN CHINESE

½ lb. Chinese noodles
4 c. cooked chicken
½ c. mushrooms (drained)
¼ c. butter or margarine
1 8-oz. can water chestnuts (drained)
1 c. grated cheese
2 eggs (well beaten)
1½ c. milk
1 t. salt
1 10½-oz. can cream of celery soup
1 c. crushed corn flakes

Grease inside of a foil tray well. Place Chinese noodles on bottom. Top with chicken, mushrooms, butter, chestnuts, and cheese. Combine eggs, milk, salt, and soup. Mix well. Pour soup mixture over top. Makes 5 to 6 servings.

Briquet Covered Cooking Method: Cover and barbecue over indirect medium heat for 45 minutes. Sprinkle corn flakes on top. Makes 5 to 6 servings.

Briquet Covered Cooking Method: Cover and barbecue over indirect medium heat for 45 minutes. Sprinkle corn flakes on top. Barbecue 15 minutes longer, uncovered.

Gas Method: Cover and barbecue over indirect medium heat for 45 minutes. Sprinkle corn flakes on top. Barbecue 15 minutes longer, uncovered.

STEAK BEAN DISH

8 strips bacon
1 medium onion, chopped
1 lb. round steak, cubed
3 beef bouillon cubes
1 c. boiling water
2 1-lb. cans pork and beans
½ c. catsup

Fry bacon, drain and cut up. Sauté onion and steak in 4 tablespoons bacon drippings. Dissolve bouillon cubes in water. Combine all ingredients. Grease aluminum foil pan. Put bean mixture into pan. Cover. Makes 6 to 7 servings.

Briquet Covered Cooking Method: Barbecue over medium indirect heat for 1 hour.

Gas Method: Barbecue over medium indirect heat for 1 hour.

MULTIMEAT LOAF

1 c. cooked veal
1 c. cooked chicken
1 c. cooked ham
2 eggs, slightly beaten
½ c. dried bread crumbs
1 T. chopped onion
2 t. salt
½ t. pepper
1 c. chicken broth or bouillon
¼ t. baking soda
Milk or cream if needed

Cut all meat into bite-size pieces. Mix all ingredients together thoroughly. Add milk if needed to moisten. Allow to rest 1 hour. Pour into well greased baking dish. Makes 6 to 7 servings.

Briquet Covered Cooking or Gas Method: Barbecue over medium/low indirect heat for 1¼ to 1½ hours or until dry.

Photograph opposite:
Brats in Beer and Beans

BOLOGNA RING

1 ring of bologna
2 c. whipped potatoes
3 slices processed American cheese

Briquet Covered Cooking or Gas Method:
Barbecue ring of bologna over medium direct heat 20 to 25 minutes. Cut 6 to 8 diagonal slits across top. Place bologna in baking dish. Fill center of ring with mashed potatoes and top with cheese slices. Barbecue 10 minutes or until cheese is melted. Makes 5 to 6 servings.

CHICKEN SUPPER

2½ to 3 lbs. cut-up chicken
2 to 3 c. diced potatoes
1 t. salt
½ t. pepper
1 c. water
2 chicken bouillon cubes

Briquet Covered Cooking or Gas Method:
Barbecue chicken over medium indirect heat for 30 minutes. Turn frequently. Remove and place in baking dish. Add potatoes, salt, pepper, and bouillon dissolved in water. Barbecue 1 hour longer. Add water if needed. Makes 5 to 6 servings.

VEAL EN CASSEROLE

2 lb. boneless veal roast
3 to 4 carrots, sliced
2 large onions, thickly sliced
3 to 4 medium potatoes, sliced
   Salt and pepper
1 t. marjoram
   White Wine Marinade, p. 56
2 medium-sized tomatoes

Place boneless roast and vegetables into baking dish. Season with marjoram, salt, and pepper. Pour White Wine Marinade over roast and vegetables. Cover. Marinate overnight. Makes 5 to 6 servings.

Briquet Covered Cooking and Gas Method:
Barbecue over medium indirect heat for 2½ hours or until meat is tender. Skin and quarter tomatoes. Add to veal/vegetable mixture. Barbecue ½ hour longer.

SCALLOPED CRAB AND CORN

1 lb. crab meat
1 1-lb. 1-oz. can whole kernel corn (with juice)
1 T. chopped chive
1 c. dried bread crumbs
2 eggs (slightly beaten)
2 T. melted butter
   Salt and pepper
   Milk if needed

Combine all ingredients. (Add a little milk if mixture seems dry.) Place into well greased baking dish. Makes 5 to 6 servings.

Briquet Covered Cooking or Gas Method:
Barbecue over medium indirect heat 30 to 40 minutes or until top is firm to touch.

SCALLOPED POTATOES AND HAM

2 T. margarine
2 T. flour
1 t. salt
¼ t. pepper
2 c. milk
4 c. thinly sliced potatoes
1 c. sliced carrots
¼ c. chopped onion
¼ c. chopped green pepper
2 c. cubed ham
8 slices Cheddar cheese

Melt margarine; stir in flour, salt, and pepper, blending well, slowly add milk. Cook over medium heat until thickened. Grease the inside of an aluminum foil pan. Put in half the ham and vegetables. Cover with half of the white sauce. Repeat with second layer. Top with cheese. Cover. Makes 5 to 6 servings.

Briquet Covered Cooking Method: Barbecue over indirect medium heat for 1 hour.

Gas Method: Barbecue over indirect medium heat for 1 hour.

EGGPLANT AND CELERY CASSEROLE

3 c. celery
3 c. eggplant
4 slices cubed fresh bread
2 beaten eggs
1 c. milk
2 T. butter or margarine
1 onion, chopped
¼ c. grated cheese

Mix all ingredients. Place in well greased aluminum foil pan. Cover. Makes 6 to 7 servings.

Briquet Covered Cooking Method: Barbecue over indirect medium heat for 30 to 35 minutes.

Gas Method: Barbecue over indirect medium heat for 30 to 35 minutes.

STROGANOFF

1 lb. round steak
½ c. chopped onion
2 4-oz. cans mushroom pieces (drained)
½ t. salt
¼ t. pepper
⅔ c. milk
1 8-oz. pkg. cream cheese

Barbecue round steak over direct heat. Remove and slice into 2-inch squares. Place into baking dish. Add onions, mushrooms, salt, pepper, and milk. Barbecue for 10 minutes. Cut cream cheese into ½-inch cubes. Add to milk mixture. Stir. Barbecue over medium heat until cheese is melted and mixture is thickened. Serve over noodles. Makes 4 to 5 servings.

SOUTH OF-THE-BORDER CASSEROLE

1 clove garlic, minced
1 medium-size onion, finely chopped
3 T. butter
1 c. tomato sauce
2 T. chili powder
1 t. salt
1 lb. boneless chuck, cut in 1-inch cubes
1 12-oz. can whole corn, drained
1 c. grated Cheddar cheese
　Grated cheese, grated onion, and shredded lettuce
　Sour cream

Sauté garlic and onion in butter until golden. Add tomato sauce, chili powder, and salt. In a large foil baking pan, layer meat, corn, and grated cheese; cover with tomato sauce mixture. Barbecue as directed. Serve garnished with grated cheese, onion, and shredded lettuce. Top wth a dollop of sour cream. Serves 4.

Briquet Covered Cooking Method: Barbecue over medium heat for 2 hours.

SNAPPER, SOLE AND SHRIMP STEW

1 T. lemon juice
1½ to 2 c. water
1 t. salt
½ t. white pepper
1 T. cornstarch
½ c. white wine
2 lbs. red snapper
2 lbs. fillet of sole
1 lb. cleaned shrimp
½ c. onion chunks
½ c. celery cubes

Combine lemon juice, water, salt, white pepper, and cornstarch. Cook over low heat until clear and thickened. Cool. Add white wine. Cut red snapper and sole into 1½ to 2-inch squares. Place snapper, sole, shrimp, and vegetables into well buttered baking dish. Pour wine mixture over top. Makes 6 to 7 servings.

Briquet Covered Cooking or Gas Method: Barbecue over medium indirect heat 20 to 25 minutes or until fish is tender. Serve over rice.

BAKED BEANS

1 2-lb. can pork and beans
½ c. catsup
3 T. dark brown sugar
2 t. prepared mustard
4 bacon slices

In a large aluminum foil pan, combine all ingredients except bacon. Lay bacon slices on top. Serves 8.

Briquet Covered Cooking or Gas Method: Barbecue over medium indirect or direct heat 1 hour or until bacon is done.

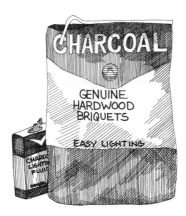

PIZZA CASSEROLE

1½ lbs. ground beef
1 c. tomato sauce
½ c. oatmeal
½ c. chopped onion
1 egg
1 T. Worcestershire sauce
1½ t. oregano
½ t. garlic powder
1 pkg. sliced mozzarella cheese

Combine all ingredients except cheese. Mix well. Pat 1/3 of meat mixture into loaf size aluminum foil pan. Top with cheese. Repeat layers saving 1/3 of cheese for last 5 minutes of barbecuing. Makes 4 to 5 servings.

Briquet Covered Cooking Method: Barbecue over medium indirect heat, uncovered, for 1 hour. Top with reserved cheese last 5 minutes of cooking time.

Gas Method: Barbecue over medium indirect heat, uncovered, for 1 hour. Top with reserved cheese last 5 minutes of cooking time.

Photograph opposite:
Pizza Casserole

BACKYARD CLAMBAKE

On a 24-inch piece of heavy-duty aluminum foil, place 1 large frozen lobster tail, 1 chicken leg, 6 clams, 1 ear of corn (silk removed), 1 scrubbed potato, 1 onion, and ½ cup clam juice. Bring up sides of foil and seal with a double fold. Double-fold ends. Place bundle, seam side down, on a second sheet of heavy-duty foil. Wrap and seal with a double fold. Each bundle serves 1.

Briquet Covered Cooking Method: Place bundles on grill 4 inches from coals. Cook 1 hour, turning every 15 minutes. Serve with melted butter and lemon.

MEALS IN A BUNDLE

2 lbs. lean chuck, cut into 1-inch cubes
6 medium potatoes, peeled and diced
6 T. chopped onion
6 carrots, sliced
½ c. chopped parsley
2 10½-oz. cans cream of mushroom soup
    Salt and pepper to taste

Divide ingredients into 6 equal portions. Place each portion on an 18-inch square of heavy-duty aluminum foil. Add 1 tablespoon water to each portion. Bring up corners of foil and twist at top to close bundles. Barbecue bundles over medium direct heat 1 hour or until potatoes and meat are tender. Serves 6.

Salads

HOT GERMAN POTATO SALAD

- 6 slices crisp bacon, diced
- ½ c. bacon drippings
- 2 T. flour
- 3 T. sugar
- 1½ t. salt
- ½ c. vinegar
- ½ c. water
- 8 medium-size potatoes, cooked and sliced
- 1 small onion, finely chopped
- 2 stalks celery, chopped

To bacon drippings, add flour, sugar, and salt; cook until bubbly. Stir in vinegar and water. Cook, stirring constantly, until thick. Cook 10 minutes over low heat. Layer one-third of the potatoes, onion, celery, bacon, and sauce; repeat for 2 more layers. Serve warm. Serves 6.

SHRIMP SALAD

- 1 small can shrimp
- 1 c. diced celery
- ¾ c. sliced stuffed olives
- 1 c. mayonnaise

Cut shrimp in small pieces; add celery and olives, mixing well. Add mayonnaise and mix. Serve on lettuce. Serves 2.

TOMATO AND CUCUMBER SALAD

- 5 medium tomatoes, sliced
- 1 cucumber, thinly sliced
- 1 green onion, thinly sliced
- 3 T. olive oil
- 2 to 3 T. red wine vinegar
- ½ t. salt
- ½ t. crushed oregano
- ¼ t. crushed basil
  Freshly ground pepper
- 1 T. minced parsley

Place tomato, cucumber, and green onion in a glass bowl. Mix together remaining ingredients and pour over salad. Chill about one hour before serving. Serves 6.

MOLDED PEAR SALAD

- 1½ c. boiling water
- 1 3-oz. pkg. lime gelatin
- ¼ c. lemon juice
- 2 c. diced pears
  Mayonnaise

Dissolve gelatin in boiling water. Add lemon juice. Set aside until slightly thickened. Fold in pears. Pour into a 3½-cup mold; chill until set. Unmold and serve with mayonnaise. Serves 8.

RED AND GREEN COLESLAW

- 3 c. shredded green cabbage
- 1 c. shredded red cabbage
- ¼ c. chopped green pepper
- ¼ c. grated onion
- 1 t. salt
- 3 t. celery seed
- 3 T. white vinegar
- ¾ c. mayonnaise

In a large bowl, combine cabbages, green pepper, and onion. Set aside. Combine remaining ingredients, mixing well. Pour over vegetables and mix well. Serves 6.

SPINACH SALAD WITH BACON DRESSING

- 6 slices crisp bacon, diced
- ½ c. bacon drippings
- 3 hard-boiled eggs
- ½ lb. fresh spinach
- 1 small onion, thinly sliced
- 1 large tomato, diced
- ½ c. white vinegar
- 1 T. sugar
- 1 t. salt
- ½ t. pepper

Chop 2 eggs; slice remaining egg for garnish. Tear spinach into bite-size pieces; mix with bacon, chopped egg, onion, and tomato. Combine bacon drippings with vinegar, sugar, salt, and pepper. Bring to a boil, stirring constantly. Pour over salad; add diced bacon and toss lightly. Garnish with egg slices. Serves 8.

OVERNIGHT SALAD

1 head lettuce, thinly sliced
1 c. chopped celery
2 3-oz. cans sliced water chestnuts
1 green pepper, chopped
1 1-lb. can small peas, drained
1 c. mayonnaise
4 T. grated Cheddar cheese

Layer lettuce, celery, water chestnuts, green pepper, and peas. Spread mayonnaise on top and sprinkle with cheese. Refrigerate overnight. Serves 6.

MELON FRUIT SALAD

1 cantaloupe
1 honeydew melon
⅓ watermelon
4 bananas
4 oranges
2 qts. strawberries
2 c. pineapple juice

Prepare melons by forming melon balls. Slice bananas and strawberries and chop oranges. Mix well with pineapple juice. Serves 8.

THREE BEAN SALAD

1 1-lb. can cut green beans
1 1-lb. can cut wax beans
1 1-lb. can kidney beans
1 1-lb. can white corn
¼ c. pimiento, chopped
1 medium onion, thinly sliced
½ c. vinegar
½ c. sugar
1 t. salt

Combine all vegetables and set aside. Slowly stir vinegar into sugar and salt, mixing to a smooth thin paste. Pour over vegetables and mix well. Let marinate overnight, stirring occasionally. Serves 8.

POTATO SALAD

3 c. cubed, boiled potatoes
½ c. thinly sliced celery
½ t. salt
3 hard-boiled eggs, chopped
¼ c. grated onion
8 slices crisp bacon, crumbled
¼ c. sliced pimiento
¼ c. sliced stuffed olives
3 t. celery seed
1 T. dill pickle juice
1 c. mayonnaise

In a large bowl, combine all ingredients except mayonnaise. Add mayonnaise and toss lightly. Serves 6.

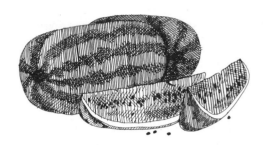

SALAD BASICS

Head lettuce
Bibb lettuce
Escarole
Romaine
Curly endive
Leaf lettuce
Boston lettuce
Watercress
Celery lettuce
Spinach

SALAD ADDITIONS

Sliced water chestnuts
Croutons browned in garlic butter
Chopped raw asparagus bits
Artichoke hearts
Crisp bacon, crumbled
Sliced fresh mushrooms
Ripe or stuffed olives, sliced
Anchovies
Hard-boiled eggs, sliced

Bread

WHITE BREAD

1 loaf frozen white bread dough

Thaw bread as stated on package. Place in a well greased red clay dish. Rise to double in bulk. Barbecue over medium moist indirect heat for 40 to 50 minutes or until golden brown. Butter top. Makes 1 loaf.

ROUND FRENCH BREAD

1 pkg. yeast
1 T. sugar
¾ t. salt
1½ c. warm water
4 c. flour

Dissolve yeast, sugar, and salt in warm water. Allow to rest 10 minutes. Add flour; stir. (Dough will be stiff.) Cover and put in a warm place for 1 hour. Stir every 15 minutes. Divide in half and place in well greased red clay dishes. Let rise 1½ hours. Barbecue 1 loaf at a time over medium/high moist heat for 35 to 40 minutes or until golden brown. Butter top for soft crust. Makes 1 loaf.

APPLE BREAD

1¾ c. flour
1 t. salt
2 t. baking powder
½ t. baking soda
1 t. cinnamon
½ t. nutmeg
½ c. shortening
½ c. brown sugar
2 eggs
1 c. grated raw apple
¼ c. milk
¼ t. vinegar

Combine all ingredients, mixing well. Pour into a well greased red clay dish. Barbecue over medium moist indirect heat for 50 to 60 minutes or until firm to the touch. Makes 1 loaf.

OATMEAL BREAD

1 c. quick rolled oats
1 c. flour
1 c. milk
1 egg
3 t. baking powder
1 t. baking soda
½ t. salt
2 T. vegetable oil

Grind oatmeal in blender. Combine all ingredients. Pour into a well greased red clay dish. Barbecue over medium indirect heat 40 to 50 minutes or until firm to the touch. Makes 1 loaf.

INDIAN BREAD

1 T. shortening (heaping)
1 c. warm water
1 t. salt
1 t. sugar
2 t. baking powder
1 t. baking soda
2 to 3 c. flour

Melt shortening in warm water. Add salt, sugar, baking powder, and baking soda. Beat in 1 to 1¼ cups flour to make batter. Stir in enough flour to make dough thick and elastic. Knead for 15 to 20 minutes using remaining flour if needed. To shape dough: roll dough in form of a ball. Make hole in center with fingers. Pull apart to doughnut shape. Place in well greased red clay dish. Slash around edge 6 times. Barbecue over medium indirect moist heat 50 to 60 minutes or until golden brown. Butter for softer crust. Makes 1 loaf.

Photograph opposite:
Indian Bread

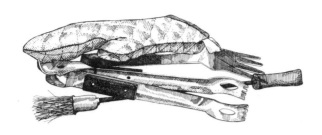

SWEET STUFFING

3 c. dried bread cubes
½ c. melted butter or margarine
½ c. chopped celery
½ c. chopped apple
1 c. seedless raisins
Warm orange juice to moisten

Combine all ingredients thoroughly. Place in a greased aluminum foil pan or use as stuffing. Makes 3 cups.

Briquet Covered Cooking or Gas Method: Barbecue for 1 hour or until dry.

CELERY STUFFING

4 stalks chopped celery
½ c. melted butter or margarine
1 onion, chopped
2 c. dried bread cubes
2 apples, chopped
1 t. sage
Salt and pepper

Combine all ingredients. Add warm water until moistened. Place in a greased aluminum foil pan or use as stuffing. Makes 1½ cups.

Briquet Covered Cooking or Gas Method: Barbecue for 1 hour or until dry.

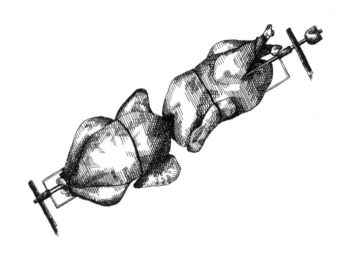

SWEET SOUR STUFFING

4 c. dry bread cubes
1 onion, finely chopped
1 t. salt
½ t. pepper
1 t. (heaping) poultry seasoning
½ c. melted butter
½ c. chopped mushroom
1 apple, finely chopped

Combine all ingredients. Moisten with diluted orange juice. Place in greased aluminum foil pan or use as stuffing. Makes 3 to 3½ cups.

Briquet Covered Cooking and Gas Method: Barbecue for 1 hour or until dry.

ALMOND MUSHROOM STUFFING

3 c. dried bread cubes
Warm water
2 T. butter or margarine
1 onion, chopped
½ c. chopped celery
⅓ c. chopped almonds
1 8-oz. can mushroom pieces (drained)
Salt and pepper
2 eggs (slightly beaten)

Cover bread cubes with warm water. Soak for 1 hour. Melt butter in pan. Add onion, celery, almonds, and mushrooms. Sauté over low heat for 5 minutes. Drain bread thoroughly. Add vegetables, salt, pepper, and eggs. Mix well. Place in a greased baking dish or use as stuffing. Barbecue over medium indirect heat for 1 hour or until dry. Makes 3 cups.

Vegetables

POTATO STICKS

1 medium potato per person
  Salt and pepper

Cut potatoes into medium size strips. Soak in ice water 1 hour. Remove; dry thoroughly. Sprinkle with salt and pepper. Place in well greased aluminum foil. Wrap securely.

Briquet Covered Cooking or Gas Method: Barbecue over medium indirect or direct heat for 50 to 60 minutes. Turn frequently.

CANDIED CARROTS

¾ c. water
3 T. brown sugar
1 T. cornstarch
½ t. salt
2 T. butter or margarine
1 1-lb. can baby carrots

Mix water, brown sugar, cornstarch, and salt. Cook over low heat until clear and slightly thickened. Add butter. Place carrots in well greased aluminum foil pan. Pour brown sugar mixture over. Makes 4 to 5 servings.

Briquet Covered Cooking or Gas Method: Barbecue over medium indirect heat for 20 minutes.

HASH BROWN POTATOES

3 c. thawed frozen hash browns
¼ c. chopped chives
½ c. chopped green pepper
1 10½-oz. can cream of celery soup
1 c. milk
  Salt and pepper
  Butter

Combine all ingredients. Grease aluminum foil pan. Place potato mixture in pan. Dot with butter. Makes 5 to 6 servings.

Briquet Covered Cooking Method: Barbecue over medium indirect heat for 1 hour.

Gas Method: Barbecue over medium indirect heat for 1 hour.

ACORN SQUASH

½ squash per person
1 T. brown sugar per ½ squash
2 T. butter per ½ squash

Cut squash in half lengthwise. Remove seeds. Put brown sugar and butter in each half. Wrap in aluminum foil. Barbecue over direct or indirect heat for 50 to 60 minutes depending on size.

ALL VEGETABLE DISH

1 c. sliced carrots
1 c. sliced celery
1 c. peas
1 c. sliced green beans
1 c. sliced yellow beans
1 10½-oz. can cream of mushroom soup
1 c. milk
  Salt and pepper

Combine all ingredients. Mix well. Place in a greased aluminum foil pan. Cover. Makes 10 to 12 servings.

Briquet Covered Cooking Method: Barbecue over medium indirect heat for 50 to 60 minutes.

Gas Method: Barbecue over medium indirect heat for 50 to 60 minutes.

GREEN BEAN AND CARROT MIX

1 10½-oz. can green beans
1 1-lb. can sliced carrots
1 t. sugar
½ t. salt
¼ c. chopped onion
1 10½-oz. can cream of celery soup
1 c. milk
  Salt and pepper

Combine all ingredients. Mix well. Place in well greased aluminum foil pan. Cover. Makes 6 to 8 servings.

Briquet Covered Cooking or Gas Method: Barbecue over medium indirect heat for 50 to 60 minutes.

CAULIFLOWER AND PEAS

½ head cauliflower
1 1-lb. can sweet peas (drained)
½ t. salt
½ c. evaporated milk
5 slices processed American cheese

Wash cauliflower thoroughly. Separate into flowerets. Boil in salted water 10 minutes. Drain. Place in a well greased baking dish; add peas and salt. Pour evaporated milk over vegetables. Top with cheese. Cover. Makes 5 to 6 servings.

Briquet Covered Cooking or Gas Method: Barbecue over medium indirect heat for 30 minutes or until cheese has melted.

CORN ON THE COB

1 to 2 ears of corn per person
Butter
Salt and pepper

Spread each ear of corn with butter; season with salt and pepper. Wrap each ear in aluminum foil.

Briquet Covered Cooking or Gas Method: Barbecue over medium direct heat for 20 minutes. Turn frequently.

ITALIAN CABBAGE

4 c. shredded cabbage
½ t. salt
Italian Sauce, p. 53
2 T. butter or margarine

Steam cabbage with small amount of water for 10 minutes. Drain thoroughly. Salt; toss to mix completely. Sprinkle with Italian Sauce. Marinate at least 2 hours. Stir occasionally. Pour into well greased baking dish. Dot with butter. Makes 5 to 6 servings.

Briquet Covered Cooking or Gas Method: Barbecue over medium indirect heat for 40 to 50 minutes.

Note: Cabbage will be crispy.

POTATO BOATS AU GRATIN

½ to ¾ c. hot whipped potatoes per person
1 t. chopped chives
Butter or margarine
1 T. grated cheese

Mix chives with whipped potatoes. Fill well-greased aluminum foil boats with whipped potatoes. Dot with butter. Top with grated cheese.

Briquet Covered Cooking or Gas Method: Barbecue over medium indirect or direct heat for 3 to 4 minutes or until cheese melts.

CANDIED YAMS

1 1-lb. can yams
½ c. brown sugar
2 T. melted butter
¼ c. honey

Drain yams, reserving juice. Place yams in a well greased aluminum foil pan. Combine yam juice, brown sugar, butter, and honey. Mix well. Pour over yams. Makes 4 to 5 servings.

Briquet Covered Cooking or Gas Method: Barbecue over medium indirect heat for 20 to 30 minutes.

FANCY GREEN BEANS

2 15½-oz. cans French style green beans
1 8-oz. can sliced water chestnuts
2 T. butter
1 10½-oz. can cream of mushroom soup
1 3-oz. can French fried onion rings
½ c. grated cheese

Combine beans, chestnuts, butter, and soup. Mix well. Grease aluminum foil pan. Pour bean mixture into pan. Top with onion rings and cheese. Makes 6 to 7 servings.

Briquet Covered Cooking Method: Barbecue over low indirect heat for 30 to 40 minutes.

Gas Method: Barbecue over low indirect heat for 30 to 40 minutes.

Photograph opposite:
Candied Yams and Fancy Green Beans

VEGETABLE KEBABS

⅓ c. brown sugar
¼ t. ginger
½ c. soy sauce
1 lb. whole fresh green beans
6 carrots, cut into thin long slices
24 paper-thin slices of sirloin or round steak

Stir soy sauce into brown sugar and ginger; marinate meat slices several hours. Parboil carrots and blanch beans. Wrap one slice meat around two beans and 2 carrot sticks. Secure on 2 thin skewers. Serves 6.

Briquet Covered Cooking Method: Barbecue over medium direct or indirect heat about 6 minutes or just until meat is done.

SQUASH ON A STICK

Zucchini or crookneck squash
Melted butter
Salt and pepper

Use very small squash or cut larger ones in 2-inch chunks. Place on long skewers. Salt and pepper to taste.

Briquet Covered Cooking or Gas Method: Barbecue over medium direct or indirect heat, basting frequently with butter, for about 20 minutes or until squash is tender.

CHEESY TOMATOES

4 tomatoes, halved
  Salt and pepper to taste
⅓ c. bread crumbs
1 c. shredded Cheddar cheese
4 T. melted butter

Season tomato halves with salt and pepper. Combine bread crumbs and cheese. Pour melted butter over, mixing well. Sprinkle cheese mixture over tomatoes. Wrap tomatoes in a double thickness of aluminum foil, sealing edges. Serves 4.

Briquet Covered Cooking or Gas Method: Barbecue over medium indirect or direct heat for about 8 to 10 minutes or until tomatoes are heated through and cheese is melted.

VEGETABLE PACKETS

6 medium-size potatoes, quartered
6 small, whole white onions
6 raw carrots, cut into 1½-inch chunks
12 whole mushrooms
12 T. butter
  Hickory smoke salt
  Pepper

Set aside 6 squares of double-thick aluminum foil, each 12 inches square. Divide vegetables between the foil squares. Place 2 tablespoons butter on top of each packet of vegetables, season with hickory smoke salt and pepper. Bring edges of foil together and fold over twice, sealing all ends. Serves 6.

Briquet Covered Cooking or Gas Method: Barbeque over indirect or direct heat 1½ hours or until potatoes are tender.

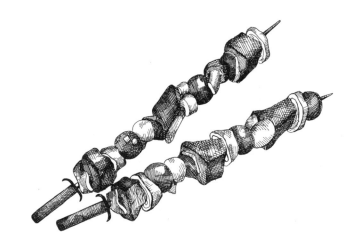

FOIL ROASTED ONIONS

6 medium-size onions
6 T. butter
  Salt, pepper, and paprika to taste

Peal and slice onions. Place onion slices on a double thickness of aluminum foil which is large enough to cover onions. Place butter on top. Sprinkle with salt, pepper, and paprika. Bring edges of foil together and fold over to close. Serves 6.

Briquet Covered Cooking or Gas Method: Barbecue over medium direct or indirect heat 20 minutes or until tender.

Marinades, Glazes, Sauces, and Relishes

SWEET MUSTARD SAUCE

¼ c. butter
2 t. flour
½ c. milk
3 T. yellow prepared mustard
2 t. sugar
2 t. brown sugar
1 t. vinegar

Over low heat, melt butter. Blend in flour to make paste. Gradually add milk to make a cream sauce. Add mustard, sugars, and vinegar. Stir constantly to medium consistency. Add more milk if needed. Makes ½ to ¾ cup.

BARBECUE SAUCE I

1 10½-oz. can tomato soup
1 c. brown sugar
4 T. butter
4 T. catsup
2 T. prepared mustard
1 t. onion powder
¼ t. garlic powder
2 T. lemon juice
1 T. Worcestershire sauce
2 T. liquid smoke

Combine all ingredients in a saucepan. Simmer until mixture comes to a boil, stirring frequently. Let simmer 1 minute. Use as a zesty sauce for beef or pork. Makes about 2 cups.

BARBECUE SAUCE II

1 medium-size onion, chopped
2 T. butter
2 T. vinegar
2 T. brown sugar
4 T. lemon juice
1 c. catsup
½ c. chopped parsley
1½ t. prepared mustard
½ c. water
3 T. Worcestershire sauce
Salt

Sauté onion in butter until golden. Add remaining ingredients; simmer 30 minutes. Use on beef, pork, or ham. Makes about 1 cup.

ITALIAN

1 c. chopped onion
3 T. vegetable oil
2 c. chopped tomatoes
½ t. garlic powder
½ t. oregano
1 bay leaf
2 whole cloves
¼ t. cinnamon
1 t. brown sugar
½ c. red wine

Sauté onion in oil until transparent. Add remaining ingredients. Cover. Simmer for 30 minutes. Remove bay leaf and cloves. Mix sauce well in blender. (Use on beef.) Makes 1½ cups.

LEMON

½ c. vegetable or olive oil
¼ c. lemon juice
1 t. ground oregano
¼ t. sweet marjoram
¼ t. dried onion flakes
½ t. paprika
Salt and pepper

Combine all ingredients in blender and mix well. (Use on poultry, fish or lamb.) Makes ¾ to 1 cup.

CURRY SAUCE

2 c. lamb broth
3 T. curry powder
3 T. dried onion flakes
2 t. garlic powder
½ c. lemon juice
½ c. grated coconut
1 c. evaporated milk
3 T. sugar
1 c. apple juice
½ c. raisins
1 T. cornstarch

Combine all ingredients. Cook over low heat, stirring frequently until thickened. Allow to stand overnight before using. Makes 2¼ cups.

MINT SAUCE

2 T. cider vinegar
¼ c. white syrup
2 t. mint extract
1 T. brown sugar
1 t. lemon juice
2 T. water

Combine all ingredients. Mix well. Makes ½ cup.

PLUM

¼ c. chopped onion
3 t. vegetable or peanut oil
2 c. water
4 T. lemon juice
½ c. plum jelly or jam
3 t. sugar
1 t. salt

Sauté onion in oil until transparent. Add remaining ingredients. Cook over medium heat for 10 minutes. Mix well in blender. (Use on poultry, lamb or veal.) Makes 2½ cups.

ORANGE SAUCE

1 chicken bouillon cube
2 T. brown sugar
¼ t. nutmeg
½ c. water
¾ c. orange juice
5 T. olive oil
1 4-oz. can mushroom pieces (drained)
½ c. dry white wine

Dissolve chicken bouillon cube, brown sugar, and nutmeg in ½ cup hot water. Cool. Combine orange juice, olive oil, mushrooms, and bouillon mixture in a blender. Blend thoroughly to purée mushrooms. Pour into small bowl. Add wine. Mix well. Cover. Refrigerate 2 to 3 days before using. Makes 1 cup.

SWEET

1 c. water
2 c. sugar
½ c. brown sugar
¼ t. cinnamon
⅛ t. nutmeg

Combine all ingredients in saucepan. Cook over medium heat until sugars are dissolved and slightly thickened (about 7 to 10 minutes). (Use on ham or pork.) Makes 2½ cups.

CRANBERRY ORANGE RELISH

2 c. grated cranberries
1 c. sugar
½ grated orange with peel
1 T. melted butter

Combine all ingredients and mix well. Place in a small buttered baking dish. Barbecue over indirect or direct heat for 10 minutes. Serves 10 to 12.

BEET RELISH

1 1-lb. can sliced beets (drained)
1 t. garlic salt
1 T. sugar
⅓ c. vinegar

Combine vinegar, garlic salt, and sugar in a small saucepan; heat. Pour over beets. Marinate overnight. Chill thoroughly before serving. Serves 10 to 12.

PEA AND ONION RELISH

1 pkg. frozen peas (thawed)
1 small onion, chopped
½ t. cornstarch
2 T. vinegar
2 T. sugar
½ t. salt

Cook peas and onion in small amount of water until slightly tender. Drain; save liquid. Dissolve cornstarch in vinegar. To reserved pea liquid add sugar, salt, and vinegar-cornstarch mixture. Cook over low heat until clear and thickened. Add peas and onion. Mix to coat. Chill. Serves 10 to 15.

Photograph opposite:
Pea and Onion Relish
Bacon Wrapped Weiners, p. 29

54

CHERRY SAUCE AND GLAZE

1 1-lb. 13-oz. can cherry pie filling
½ can water

Combine pie filling and water. Use as glaze on pork or ham. Serve remaining with meal. Makes 4 cups.

PINEAPPLE GLAZE

1 c. pineapple juice or juice from pineapple slices or chunks
½ c. cider vinegar
¼ c. black molasses
2 T. maraschino cherry juice
1 T. brown sugar
1 T. cornstarch

Combine pineapple juice, vinegar, molasses, cherry juice, and brown sugar in saucepan. Mix well. Blend in cornstarch. Cook over low heat, stirring constantly until thickened. Makes 1½ cups.

BEEF BOUILLON MARINADE

2 small onions, chopped
2 T. shortening
1 c. water
3 beef bouillon cubes
¼ t. garlic powder
1 c. tomato juice
2 t. salt
1 T. Worcestershire sauce

Sauté onion in shortening until transparent. Add remaining ingredients. Cover. Simmer for 15 minutes. Makes 2½ cups.

BEER MARINADE

1 large onion, chopped
2 c. flat beer
⅛ t. ginger

Combine ingredients in blender. Mix thoroughly. Makes 2 cups.

SOY MARINADE

⅓ c. vegetable oil
5 T. soy sauce
2 T. catsup
1 t. garlic
1 T. vinegar
1 T. Worcestershire sauce
Dash of black pepper

Combine all ingredients and mix well. Makes ½ cup.

RED WINE MARINADE

1 c. dry red wine
½ c. salad oil
⅛ t. marjoram
⅛ t. rosemary
⅛ t. basil
⅛ t. dried parsley

Combine all ingredients in blender. Mix well. Makes 1½ cups.

WHITE WINE MARINADE

1 c. white wine
½ c. salad oil
½ t. celery salt
¼ t. dried onion
¼ t. black pepper
1 t. marjoram
1 t. thyme

Combine all ingredients in blender. Mix well. Makes 1½ cups.

The Finishing Touches

BLUEBERRY DUMPLINGS

1 large can blueberry pie filling
¼ to ½ c. water
1 pkg. refrigerated biscuits

Mix water with blueberry pie filling. Pour into greased baking dish. Cover with biscuits. Barbecue over medium indirect heat until biscuits are golden brown. Makes 6 to 9 servings.

HAWAIIAN DELIGHT

1 medium-size pineapple
15 whole cloves
½ c. honey

Prepare pineapple by removing leaves and peeling, cutting out "eyes." Poke whole cloves around pineapple. Serves 8.

Spit Method: Place pineapple on spit securely. Barbecue on rotating spit over medium heat for about 30 minutes, basting frequently with honey. Slice and serve.

PEACH CRISP

½ c. brown sugar
½ c. flour
½ c. butter or margarine
1 large can sliced peaches
1 t. almond extract
¼ t. nutmeg
2 T. cornstarch

Mix brown sugar, flour, and butter. Pat 2/3 of mixture into baking dish. Drain peach juice into saucepan. Add extract, nutmeg, and cornstarch. Cook over low heat until clear and thickened. Add peaches. Stir to mix. Pour filling over crumb base. Sprinkle with remaining crumbs. Barbecue over medium heat for 20 to 30 minutes. Makes 6 to 7 servings.

BAKED APPLES

4 medium-size apples
4 T. butter
4 t. cinnamon
4 t. sugar

Core apples and place 1 tablespoon butter in the top of each apple. Combine sugar and cinnamon; divide cinnamon-sugar among apples and fill core. Place each apple on a square of aluminum foil large enough to wrap around apple. Fold corners together and twist, sealing edges. Barbecue for about 45 minutes over medium-hot coals, rotating apples occasionally. Serves 4.

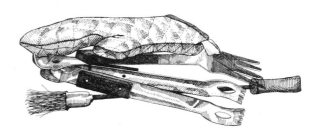

RAISIN PUDDING

½ c. shortening
½ c. sugar
¾ c. raisins
1 egg
1 c. flour
¼ t. salt
½ t. baking soda
½ t. cinnamon
¼ c. milk
1 t. vanilla

Cream shortening and sugar together. Add remaining ingredients and mix well. Pour into 6-oz. well greased custard cups (¾ full). Place in a 9-inch round baking dish. Add ½ inch water to baking dish. Barbecue over medium indirect heat until pudding is set. Add more water if needed. Makes 4 to 5 servings.

RUM ICE

¼ c. rum per person
1 t. lime juice
1 T. sugar
1 glass crushed ice

Mix rum, lime juice, and sugar. Pour over crushed ice.

CONTINENTAL COFFEE

¾ c. hot coffee per person
1 t. chocolate drink mix per cup
1 t. sugar per cup

Dissolve chocolate drink mix and sugar in hot coffee. Serve in mugs.

CHERRY-BANANA DELIGHT

1 c. frosted cereal flakes
¼ c. brown sugar
1 T. flour
3 T. melted butter or margarine
1 1-lb. 13-oz. can cherry pie filling
2 bananas, sliced

Combine cereal flakes, brown sugar, flour, and butter. Mix well. Combine cherry pie filling and banana slices. Press 2/3 of cereal flakes mixture into bottom of a greased baking dish. Pour in filling. Sprinkle remaining flake mixture over top. Barbecue over medium indirect heat for 20 to 30 minutes. Makes 6 to 9 servings.

Photograph opposite:
Cherry-Banana Delight

HOT FRUIT COMPOTE

1 large can peaches
1 large can pineapple slices
1 large can apricots
1 can dark cherries, pitted
½ c. butter
2 T. flour
¼ c. sugar
1 c. sherry

Drain all fruit, and combine in a large foil pan. In saucepan over hot coals, melt butter; stir in flour and sugar, mixing well. Slowly add sherry. Pour over fruit. Serves 6.

Briquet Covered Cooking Method or Gas Grill: Barbecue over medium heat about 15 minutes or until bubbly.

RHUBARB CREAM

1½ c. sugar
3 T. flour
½ t. grated orange peel
½ t. nutmeg
2 T. butter
2 eggs, well-beaten
3 c. cut-up rhubarb

Blend sugar, flour, orange peel, nutmeg, butter, and eggs until smooth. Place rhubarb in a well greased baking dish. Pour egg mixture over top of rhubarb. Sprinkle with your favorite crumb topping. Barbecue over medium indirect heat 40 to 50 minutes or until set. Makes 6 to 9 servings.

POPCORN

6 T. vegetable oil
6 T. popcorn
1 18-inch square aluminum foil
¼ c. melted butter
Salt to taste

Place popcorn into center of foil; pour oil over. Fold over edges and seal well. Tie to a long stick. Hold over hot coals and shake as corn begins to pop. Season popped corn with melted butter and salt.

FRUITED ICE

1 banana, sliced
1 peach, sliced
6 to 10 maraschino cherries, halved
6 to 10 miniature marshmallows
15 to 20 seedless grapes, peeled
½ c. evaporated milk
¼ c. sugar

Pour evaporated milk in refrigerator/freezer tray. Chill until ice forms around side. Whip; add sugar. Fold fruit into whipped milk. Freeze until firm. Makes 2 cups.

BERRIES AND CREAM

1 qt. strawberries
⅓ c. sugar
1 qt. red raspberries
1 c. heavy cream
¼ c. sugar

Divide strawberries among six serving dishes. In blender or food processor, purée raspberries with 1/3 cup sugar. Whip cream, sweetening with remaining sugar. Pour raspberry purée over strawberries and garnish with dollop of whipped cream.

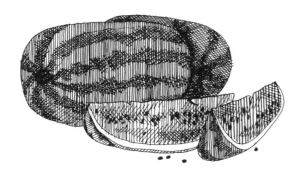

GRASSHOPPERS

1 pt. vanilla ice cream, softened
1 T. sugar
3 to 4 T. creme de menthe syrup

Whip ingredients together. Pile high in pilsner beer glasses. Makes 4 servings.

FRESH PEACH ICE CREAM

4 eggs
1¾ c. sugar
1 c. milk
5 c. peach purée
4 c. heavy cream
4½ t. vanilla
½ t. salt

Beat eggs; gradually beat in sugar. Continue beating until mixture is stiff. Stir in remaining ingredients, mixing thoroughly. Pour into 1-gallon ice cream freezer and freeze as machine directions indicate. Makes 1 gallon ice cream.

APRICOT SHERBET

1 can apricot halves with juice
1 pkg. whipped topping mix

Pour apricots with juice in blender; purée. Whip topping mix as stated on package. Whip apricot purée into whipped topping. Freeze until firm. Makes 2 cups.

CHOCOLATE ICE CREAM

5 1-oz. squares unsweetened chocolate, melted
5 c. milk
2½ c. sugar
5 T. flour
¾ t. salt
4 eggs, slightly beaten
5 c. cream
2 t. vanilla

Scald milk; stir in melted chocolate. Set aside. In a 5-quart pot, combine sugar, flour, and salt, mixing well. Stir in beaten eggs, mixing thoroughly. Slowly stir in hot chocolate-milk mixture. Simmer over low heat, stirring constantly until mixture coats spoon. Chill thoroughly. Stir in cream and vanilla. Freeze in ice cream freezer according to manufacturer's directions.

Index

Notes

G H I K L M

2 3 4 5 6 7 8 9 0 1